Congressional
Research Service
Informing the legislative debate since 1914 _____

The Palestinians: Background and U.S. Relations

Jim Zanotti
Specialist in Middle Eastern Affairs

January 31, 2014

Congressional Research Service

7-5700

www.crs.gov

RL34074

Summary

This report covers current issues in U.S.-Palestinian relations. It also contains an overview of Palestinian society and politics and descriptions of key Palestinian individuals and groups—chiefly the Palestine Liberation Organization (PLO), the Palestinian Authority (PA), Fatah, Hamas, and the Palestinian refugee population. The "Palestinian question" is important not only to Palestinians, Israelis, and their Arab state neighbors, but to many countries and non-state actors in the region and around the world—including the United States—for a variety of religious, cultural, and political reasons. U.S. policy toward the Palestinians is marked by efforts to establish a Palestinian state through a negotiated two-state solution to the Israeli-Palestinian conflict; to counter Palestinian terrorist groups; and to establish norms of democracy, accountability, and good governance in West Bank areas administered by the Fatah-led PA. Congress has appropriated assistance to support Palestinian governance and development while trying to prevent the funds from benefitting Palestinians who advocate violence against Israelis. Since the signing of the Oslo Accord in 1993, Congress has committed more than $5 billion in bilateral assistance to the Palestinians, over half of it since mid-2007.

Among the issues in U.S. policy toward the Palestinians is how to deal with the political leadership of Palestinian society, which is divided between the Fatah-led PA in parts of the West Bank and Hamas (a U.S.-designated Foreign Terrorist Organization) in the Gaza Strip. Following Hamas's takeover of Gaza in June 2007, the United States has sought to bolster the West Bank-based PA, led by President Mahmoud Abbas, who also chairs the PLO.

The United States has supported various rounds of Israeli-Palestinian negotiations for more than 20 years. While a negotiating process was lacking in 2011 and 2012, Abbas and the PLO/PA actively worked to obtain more widespread international recognition of Palestinian statehood, which triggered some temporary informal Congressional holds on U.S. aid to Palestinians. The PLO has not obtained membership in the United Nations, but a November 2012 resolution in the U.N. General Assembly identified "Palestine" as a "non-member state," and the U.N. Educational, Scientific and Cultural Organization (UNESCO) admitted "Palestine" in late 2011. Similar future Palestinian initiatives, such as those that might encourage International Criminal Court (ICC) action against Israelis, could trigger existing legal restrictions on U.S. aid and lead to greater Congressional scrutiny of future aid. However, such efforts appear to be on hold, given ongoing negotiations between Israel and the PLO that might lead to a framework document—possibly U.S.-drafted—setting the parameters for a final resolution of several disputed issues.

The Gaza situation also presents a dilemma. Humanitarian and economic problems persist, perhaps partly due to a closure regime enforced by Israel and Egypt. These two countries, the United States, and other international actors are reluctant to take direct action toward opening Gaza's borders fully because of legal, political, and strategic challenges to dealing with Hamas. Power-sharing arrangements among Palestinian factions that would allow for presidential and legislative elections and reunified PA rule over Gaza and parts of the West Bank are often proposed but remain unimplemented. Political support and economic assistance from Iran, Qatar, Turkey, and private Gulf state donors may bolster Hamas's rule and, combined with other factors, exacerbate the Palestinian political divide. Nevertheless, measures by Egypt to counter militant groups operating in the Sinai Peninsula and to curb smuggling to Gaza, on top of existing Israeli practices, have disrupted aspects of Hamas's rule. It is unclear how and to what extent Hamas might seek to strengthen its control in Gaza, to respond militarily, or to reach political accommodation.

Contents

Figures

Tables

Appendixes

Contacts

Issues for Congress

Congress plays a significant role in U.S. policy toward the Palestinians. Since the signing of the Oslo Accord in 1993, Congress has committed more than $5 billion in bilateral assistance to the Palestinians. From FY2008 to the present, annual U.S. bilateral assistance to the West Bank and Gaza Strip has averaged nearly $500 million, including annual averages of approximately $200 million in direct budgetary assistance and $100 million in non-lethal security assistance for the Palestinian Authority (PA) in the West Bank. See CRS Report RS22967, *U.S. Foreign Aid to the Palestinians*, by Jim Zanotti, for a more detailed description of this topic and the particulars of U.S. assistance and recent informal congressional holds. Congress expanded aid appropriations after PA President Mahmoud Abbas dismissed Hamas ministers from government shortly following Hamas's takeover of Gaza in 2007. The United States' counterparts in the international "Quartet" (the European Union, the United Nations Secretary-General's office, and Russia) have also sought to bolster the West Bank-based PA. Additionally, the United States remains the largest single-state donor to the U.N. Relief and Works Agency for Palestine Refugees in the Near East (UNRWA).

Some Members of Congress question the continuation of U.S. budgetary, security, and/or developmental assistance to the Palestinians. Two concerns have predominated in the past few years. First, some Members have opposed a Palestine Liberation Organization (PLO)/PA effort to pursue additional international recognition of Palestinian statehood outside negotiations with Israel, including at the United Nations. With the resumption of direct Israeli-Palestinian negotiations during the summer of 2013, the PLO/PA has halted formal initiatives for international recognition for the time being. Second, some Members have asserted that the United States should not provide assistance to the PA if a power-sharing arrangement that returns the West Bank and Gaza to unified rule is approved by Hamas. The Consolidated Appropriations Act, 2014 (P.L. 113-76), includes conditions on U.S. aid to the PA addressing these concerns, but the merits and sufficiency of these conditions remain subject to debate.

As Congress weighs the effectiveness and appropriateness of U.S. aid to the Palestinians and exercises oversight over Israeli-Palestinian developments, Members may consider the following:

- Prospects for a negotiated two-state solution between Israel and the PLO—with or without U.N. or other measures relating to Palestinian statehood.

- Threats of terrorism and armed conflict—both Israeli-Palestinian and intra-Palestinian—and options (military, political, economic) to prevent, counter, or mitigate these threats.

- The possible impact of regional developments, including leadership transitions and concerns over stability in Egypt (especially the Sinai Peninsula), Syria, Lebanon, and Jordan.

- Palestinian leadership and civil society developments, including potential power sharing among Fatah and Hamas; the likelihood of elections and concerns about growing authoritarianism in their absence; and political participation in the West Bank, Gaza, East Jerusalem, and among Palestinian refugees and diaspora members.

- The implications of initiatives by Palestinian leaders, Israel, and other international actors for Palestinians on security, political, economic, and humanitarian matters.

Overview

The "Palestinian Question," Israel, and Prospects for Peace

The Palestinians are Arabs who live in the geographical area that constitutes present-day Israel, the West Bank, and the Gaza Strip, or who have historical and/or cultural ties to that area. Since the early 20th Century, the desire to establish an independent state in historic Palestine has remained the dominant Palestinian national goal. Over time, Palestinians have differed among themselves, with Israelis, and with others over the nature and extent of such a state and the legitimacy of various means to achieve it. Today, the "Palestinian Question" focuses on whether and how Palestinians can overcome internal divisions and external opposition to establish a viable, independent state capable of fulfilling their shared national aspirations. Along with the Palestinians of the West Bank, Gaza, and East Jerusalem (which include nearly 2 million U.N.-registered refugees), nearly 3 million Palestinian U.N.-registered refugees outside these territories, in addition to a wider diaspora, await a permanent resolution of their situation.[1]

Historical Background

Historians have noted that the concept of Palestinian national identity is a relatively recent phenomenon and in large part grew from the challenge posed by increased Jewish migration to the area that now makes up Israel, the West Bank, and Gaza during the eras of Ottoman and British control in the first half of the 20th Century.[2] Palestinian political identity emerged during the British Mandate period (1923-1948), began to crystallize with the 1947 United Nations partition plan (General Assembly Resolution 181), and grew stronger following Israel's conquest and occupation of the West Bank and Gaza Strip in 1967. Although in 1947 the United Nations intended to create two states in Palestine—one Jewish and one Arab—only the Jewish state came into being. Varying explanations for the failure to found an Arab state alongside a Jewish state in mandatory Palestine place blame on the British, the Zionists, neighboring Arab states, the Palestinians themselves, or some combination of these groups.[3]

As the state of Israel won its independence in 1947-1948, roughly 700,000 Palestinians were driven or fled from their homes, an occurrence Palestinians call the *nakba* ("catastrophe"). Many from the diaspora ended up in neighboring states (Egypt, Syria, Lebanon, and Jordan) or in Gulf states such as Kuwait. Palestinians remaining in Israel became Israeli citizens. Those who were in the West Bank (including East Jerusalem) and Gaza were subject to Jordanian and Egyptian administration, respectively. With their population in disarray, and no clear hierarchical structure

---

[1] See http://www.unrwa.org/where-we-work for a place-by-place breakdown of U.N.-registered refugees.

[2] See Rashid Khalidi, *Palestinian Identity: The Construction of Modern National Consciousness,* New York: Columbia Univ. Press, 1997.

[3] See, e.g., Edward Said, *The Question of Palestine*, New York: Times Books, 1979; Barry Rubin, *Israel: An Introduction*, New Haven: Yale University Press, 2012.

or polity to govern their affairs, Palestinians' interests were largely represented by Arab states with conflicting internal and external interests.

1967 was a watershed year for the Palestinians. In the June Six-Day War, Israel decisively defeated the Arab states who had styled themselves as the Palestinians' protectors, seizing East Jerusalem, the West Bank, and the Gaza Strip (as well as the Sinai Peninsula from Egypt and the Golan Heights from Syria). Thus, Israel gained control over the entire area that constituted Palestine under the British Mandate. Israel's territorial gains provided buffer zones between Israel's main Jewish population centers and its traditional Arab state antagonists. These buffer zones remain an important part of the Israeli strategic calculus to this day.

Ultimately Israel only effectively annexed East Jerusalem (as well as the Golan Heights), leaving the West Bank and Gaza under military occupation. However, both territories became increasingly economically interdependent with Israel. Furthermore, Israel presided over the settlement of thousands of Jewish civilians in both territories (although many more in the West Bank than Gaza)—officially initiating some of these projects and assuming security responsibility for all of them. Settlement of the West Bank in particular increased markedly once the Likud Party, with its vision of a "Greater Israel" extending from the Mediterranean Sea to the Jordan River, took power in 1977. This presented some economic and cultural opportunities for Palestinians, but also new challenges to their identity, property rights, civil liberties, morale, political cohesion, and territorial contiguity. These challenges persist and have since intensified.

The Arab states' humiliation in 1967, and Israeli rule and settlement of the West Bank and Gaza, allowed the Palestine Liberation Organization (PLO) to emerge as the representative of Palestinian national aspirations. Founded in 1964 as an umbrella organization of Palestinian factions and militias in exile under the aegis of the League of Arab States (Arab League), the PLO asserted its own identity after the Six-Day War by staging guerrilla raids against Israel from Jordanian territory. Yasser Arafat and his Fatah movement gained leadership of the PLO in 1969, and the PLO subsequently achieved international prominence on behalf of the Palestinian national cause—representing both the refugees and those under Israeli rule in the West Bank and Gaza—although often this prominence came infamously from acts of terrorism and militancy.

Although Jordan forced the PLO to relocate to Lebanon in the early 1970s, and Israel forced it to move from Lebanon to Tunisia in 1982, the organization and its influence survived. In 1987, Palestinians inside the West Bank and Gaza rose up in opposition to Israeli occupation (the first *intifada*, or uprising), leading to increased international attention and sympathy for the Palestinians' situation. In December 1988, as the intifada continued, Arafat initiated dialogue with the United States by renouncing violence, promising to recognize Israel's right to exist, and accepting the "land-for-peace" principle embodied in U.N. Security Council Resolution 242.[4] Many analysts believe that Arafat's turn to diplomacy with the United States and Israel was at least partly motivated by concerns that if the PLO's leadership could not be repatriated from exile, its legitimacy with Palestinians might be overtaken by local leaders of the intifada in the West Bank and Gaza (which included Hamas). These concerns intensified when Arafat lost much

---

[4] UNSCR 242, adopted in 1967 shortly after the Six-Day War, calls for a "just and lasting peace in the Middle East" based on (1) "Withdrawal of Israeli armed forces from territories occupied in the [1967 Six-Day War]" and (2) "Termination of all claims or states of belligerency and respect for and acknowledgement of the sovereignty, territorial integrity and political independence of every State in the area and their right to live in peace within secure and recognized boundaries free from threats or acts of force."

of his Arab state support following his political backing for Saddam Hussein's 1990 invasion of Kuwait.

After direct secret diplomacy with Israel brokered by Norway, the PLO recognized Israel's right to exist in 1993, and through a succession of agreements (known as the "Oslo Accords"), gained limited self-rule for Palestinians in Gaza and parts of the West Bank—complete with democratic mechanisms; security forces; and executive, legislative, and judicial organs of governance under the PA. The Oslo Accords were gradually and partially implemented during the 1990s, but the expectation that they would lead to a final-status peace agreement has not been realized.

Many factors—including violence, leadership changes and shortcomings, rejectionist movements with sizeable popular followings (particularly Hamas on the Palestinian side), a continued Israeli security presence, expanded Israeli settlement of the West Bank and East Jerusalem, and international involvement—have contributed to the failure to complete the Oslo process. A second Palestinian intifada from 2000 to 2005 was marked by intense terrorist violence inside Israel and actions—asserted by Israel to be necessary to safeguard its citizens' security—by Israeli security forces that rendered much of the PA infrastructure built over the preceding decade unusable. During the second intifada, U.S.- and internationally supported efforts to restart peace negotiations under various auspices failed to gain traction. After Arafat's death in 2004[5] and his succession by Mahmoud Abbas, Israel unilaterally withdrew its settlers and military forces from Gaza in 2005. However, the limited self-rule regime of the PA was undermined further by Hamas's legislative election victory in 2006, and the Hamas takeover of Gaza in 2007. These developments, along with subsequent violence and regional political changes, have since increased confusion regarding questions of Palestinian leadership, territorial contiguity, and prospects for statehood.

Present and Future Considerations

Today, Fatah and Hamas are the largest Palestinian political movements (see **Appendix A** and **Appendix B** for profiles of both groups and their leaders). The positions that their leaders express reflect the two basic cleavages in Palestinian society:

1. Between those (Fatah) who seek to establish a state by nonviolent means—negotiations, international diplomacy, civil disobedience—and those (Hamas) who insist on maintaining violence as an option; and

2. Between those (Fatah) who favor a secular model of governance and those (Hamas) who seek a society governed more by Islamic norms.

---

[5] Arafat fell ill in Ramallah, West Bank, in October 2004, was transported to a military hospital in France, and died there. Records indicate that he died of a stroke resulting from a bleeding disorder caused by an unidentified underlying infection. Many Palestinians maintain that he was poisoned, with several theories blaming Israel and/or one or more of his Palestinian rivals or potential successors. Evidence revealed by Arafat's widow Suha indicating the presence of polonium on articles of Arafat's clothing led in August 2012 to French authorities opening an inquiry into his death and in November 2012 to the exhumation and reburial of his remains.

Three parties—the French probe, a Swiss medical laboratory, and a group of Russian experts appointed by the PA—have been involved in conducting tests on samples taken from Arafat's exhumed remains. Reports from these parties came out near the end of 2013, with the French team (reportedly) and the Russian team ruling out the poisoning theory and the Swiss laboratory offering "moderate backing for the theory." Palestinian officials have indicated that they will continue conducting investigations into Arafat's death. "Yasser Arafat died of natural causes - Russian report," *BBC News*, December 26, 2013.

At present, many Palestinians perceive U.S. policy to reflect a pro-Israel bias and a lack of sensitivity to PA President/PLO Chairman Mahmoud Abbas's domestic political rivalry with Hamas and other groups. These perceptions appear to stem from—among other things—U.S. efforts to prioritize the continuation of Israeli-Palestinian final-status negotiations over an Israeli settlement freeze. The United States vetoed a U.N. Security Council draft resolution condemning Israeli settlements in February 2011.[6]

During the past few years, lack of progress on the peace process with Israel has led Abbas and his colleagues to consider alternative pathways toward a Palestinian state, based on the strategy of obtaining more widespread international recognition of Palestinian statehood in the West Bank (including East Jerusalem) and the Gaza Strip. According to reports, Abbas also periodically considers—but apparently has chosen to avoid, delay, or deemphasize—other alternative strategies for the West Bank. Such alternatives include encouraging greater Palestinian nonviolent resistance to Israel and even dissolving the PA altogether.[7] Some Palestinian and international intellectuals continue to advocate the idea of a "binational" or "one-state" idea as an alternative to a negotiated two-state solution, even though polls indicate that a majority of both Israelis and Palestinians would prefer separate states and national identities.[8]

The "Palestinian question" is important not only to Palestinians, Israelis, and their Arab state neighbors, but to many countries and non-state actors in the region and around the world—including the United States—for a variety of religious, cultural, and political reasons. Over the past 66 years, if not longer, the issue has been one of the most provocative in the international arena. Al Qaeda and its affiliates, Iran, and others seeking to garner support for and/or mobilize Arab and Muslim sentiment against the United States, Israel, and/or other Western nations routinely use the Palestinian cause as a touchstone for their grievances. Analysts often debate whether the Palestinian question is truly central to the region's and world's problems, with some contending that more often than not it is used by various actors as a pretext to deflect attention from matters more central to their respective interests.

Current Israeli-Palestinian Negotiations

In late July 2013, Secretary of State John Kerry convened talks between Israeli and PLO negotiators in Washington, DC, to discuss a framework for final-status negotiations on issues of Israeli-Palestinian dispute. The discussions that subsequently began in Jerusalem in mid-August at the envoy/negotiator level are the first direct Israel-PLO negotiations since September 2010. Also in July, Kerry appointed Martin Indyk, a former U.S. Ambassador to Israel and Clinton

---

[6] All other 14 members of the Security Council voted for the draft resolution.

[7] International Crisis Group, *The Emperor Has No Clothes: Palestinians and the End of the Peace Process*, Middle East Report No. 122, May 7, 2012. Those who support the idea of dissolving the PA apparently believe that Israel's motivation for agreeing to Palestinian sovereignty in the West Bank (and possibly Gaza) might increase considerably were it to again shoulder the full burden of governing the territory and its residents. Others dismiss the plausibility of the idea, largely over concerns about possible destabilization given the direct reliance of over 150,000 Palestinians (and their families) on PA employment. The Palestinian Center for Policy and Survey Research published a series of reports in 2013 on the possibility of collapse or dissolution of the PA under the title of *The Day After: How Palestinians Can Cope if the PA Ceases to Function.*

[8] See, e.g., Abdallah Schleifer, "One-state: solution or illusion for Palestine?," *Al Arabiya*, September 25, 2013. Most scenarios envisioning a binational Israeli-Palestinian state would apparently fundamentally change or abrogate the Zionist nature of Israel's institutional and societal makeup. Such developments would by almost all accounts be unacceptable to a large majority of Israelis.

Administration official, as U.S. Special Envoy for Israeli-Palestinian Negotiations.[9] President Obama has endorsed the talks' resumption, and identified them in his September 2013 U.N. General Assembly address as one of two specific short-term priorities of U.S. diplomacy (the other being the Iranian nuclear issue).[10] Yet, it is unclear to what extent Obama plans to play a direct role. The negotiations are being conducted under a nine-month timeline—ending in April 2014—for agreement.

After some seemingly conflicting statements by Secretary Kerry in late 2013 regarding whether negotiations would focus on all issues of dispute or give priority to borders and security, media reports claim that he is seeking a framework document—possibly U.S.-drafted—that would clarify the parameters for final negotiations on several issues. Presumably in response to widespread observations that such a framework revisits the pattern of prior U.S.-backed formulas in using interim agreements as initial steps toward an elusive final resolution, on January 5, 2014, Kerry made the following statement in Jerusalem:

> I want to reiterate – we are not working on an interim agreement. We are working on a framework for negotiations that will guide and create the clear, detailed, accepted roadmap for the guidelines for the permanent status negotiations, and can help those negotiations move faster and more effectively.[11]

Many observers assert that Kerry seeks to have the parties approve a framework document by April in order to avoid a breakdown of negotiations after the original nine-month timeframe for the talks. Pushing the deadline back would provide additional time for diplomacy on the Iranian nuclear issue to develop. Greater clarification or complication on this issue could affect prospects for an Israeli-Palestinian breakthrough. The PLO agreed during the initial period of the talks to forgo formal international initiatives (such as at the United Nations) aimed at strengthening claims of Palestinian statehood. It might continue forgoing these initiatives if it perceives that a prolonged process strengthens its claims to future statehood and increases Palestinian opportunities for international political backing and economic investment. If Israel and the PLO approve a framework document, publication of its terms might make it difficult for the parties to backtrack or renege on positions to which they initially acquiesce.

Media reports indicate that substantive differences divide Israeli and Palestinian negotiators. PLO Chairman Abbas is reportedly reluctant to recognize Israel as "the nation-state of the Jewish people" because of the potential repercussions for Palestinian refugees' claim to a right of return and for Israeli Arabs' rights. Other Arab foreign ministers have reportedly informed Secretary

---

[9] The British-born, Australian-raised Indyk has served twice as Ambassador to Israel (1995-1997 and 2000-2001), and also served during the Clinton Administration as a senior Middle East official on the National Security Council and in the State Department. He was closely involved with the Oslo-era negotiations coordinated by then U.S. envoy Dennis Ross. Kerry has appointed his longtime aide Frank Lowenstein as Indyk's deputy and as a senior advisor to Kerry. Former Senator George Mitchell served as Special Envoy for Middle East Peace from 2009 (shortly after President Obama's inauguration) until his 2011 resignation, and was followed by David Hale, a career diplomat with considerable Middle East experience.

[10] White House transcript of remarks by President Obama at the U.N. General Assembly in New York, September 24, 2013.

[11] Transcript of remarks by Secretary of State John Kerry, "Remarks at Solo Press Availability," David Citadel Hotel, Jerusalem, January 5, 2014.

Kerry that they will "not accept Israel as a Jewish state nor compromise on Palestinian sovereignty in Jerusalem."[12]

Additionally, despite efforts by Kerry and a team of U.S. experts headed by retired Marine General John R. Allen[13] to bridge the divide on security arrangements in the Jordan Valley border area of the West Bank, reports assert that neither side has embraced the proposals. PLO negotiators publicly reject an extended Israeli military presence within what they assert would be sovereign Palestinian territory, while Israel may not be willing to agree to phase out its presence—largely owing to recent historical instances in which Israeli military withdrawal from southern Lebanon (2000) and the Gaza Strip (2005) led to the entrenchment of adversarial Islamist militants armed with rockets that have hit Israeli population centers and remain capable of doing so.

Contention has also persisted between the parties over possible land swaps[14] and mutual allegations of incitement and provocation.[15] To some extent, accusations the two sides levy against each other on these subjects may represent efforts to assign blame if the negotiations break down.

Prior to the renewed talks, Israel's coalition government approved the eventual release of 104 Palestinian prisoners in four tranches of 26 each. The first three tranches have taken place on schedule in August, October, and December 2013, with each closely followed by Israeli announcements relating to settlement construction. Secretary Kerry had acknowledged in August that settlement announcements might take place "within the so-called blocs in areas that many people make a presumption—obviously not some Palestinians or others—will be part of Israel in

---

[12] Elhanan Miller, "Arab ministers back Abbas in rejecting 'Jewish' Israel," *Times of Israel*, January 13, 2014. The United States sometimes seeks regional Arab support on certain positions that are domestically unpopular with Palestinians, probably in order to create political space for PLO leaders to more seriously consider accepting these positions or to apply pressure on them to do so. In April 2013, the League of Arab States agreed that land swaps could be an element of a conflict-ending agreement between Israel and the PLO. The 2002 Arab Peace Initiative offered a comprehensive Arab peace with Israel if Israel were to withdraw fully from the territories it occupied in 1967, agree to the establishment of a Palestinian state with a capital in East Jerusalem, and provide for the "[a]chievement of a just solution to the Palestinian Refugee problem in accordance with UN General Assembly Resolution 194." The initiative was proposed by then Crown Prince (now King) Abdullah of Saudi Arabia, adopted by the 22-member Arab League (which includes the PLO), and later accepted by the 56-member Organization of the Islamic Conference (now the Organization of Islamic Cooperation) at its 2005 Mecca summit. The text of the initiative is available at http://www.bitterlemons.org/docs/summit html.

[13] General Allen commanded all U.S. and U.S.-allied forces in Afghanistan from 2011 to 2013.

[14] Foreign Minister Avigdor Lieberman advocates the idea of exchanging an area of Israeli territory that has large Arab population concentrations (est. 300,000, known as the "Arab Triangle") and is adjacent to the northern West Bank for Jewish settlement blocs in the West Bank. Such an exchange, which appears to be objectionable to most Palestinians and Israeli Arabs, would decrease Israel's Arab population and apparently involve revoking the Israeli citizenship of the Triangle's residents.

[15] William Booth, "Israel says Palestinians push a 'culture of hate' that could undermine talks," *Washington Post*, January 7, 2014. A 2013 State Department-funded study of Israeli and Palestinian school books, conducted by a joint Israeli-Palestinian research team, found that books from both sides present "unilateral national narratives" and that "dehumanizing and demonizing characterizations of the other" are rare. The study is available at http://d7hj1xx5r7f3h.cloudfront net/Israeli-Palestinian_School_Book_Study_Report-English.pdf. Representative Edward Royce, Chairman of the House Foreign Affairs Committee, is sponsoring the Palestinian Peace Promotion and Anti-Incitement Act (H.R. 3868), which would condition U.S. assistance to the PA on a presidential certification that the PA "(1) no longer engages in a pattern of incitement against the United States or Israel; and (2) is engaged in peace preparation activities aimed at promoting peace with the Jewish State of Israel."

---

the future."[16] However, announcements made in January 2014 following the December 2013 prisoner release included at least one area that most observers conclude falls outside these blocs.[17]

Although Hamas's control of Gaza and the group's considerable Palestinian base of support continue to challenge Abbas's claim to be a credible "partner for peace," Hamas's regional political support appears to have declined. First, at the end of 2011, Syria's civil war distanced Hamas from Iran and the Asad regime. Then, during the summer of 2013, political transitions in Egypt and Qatar disempowered Hamas-friendly leaders in those countries, and Egypt's military operations in Sinai have disrupted aspects of Hamas's rule in Gaza, including the revenues it receives from smuggling tunnels.[18]

---

[16] Transcript of remarks by Secretary of State John Kerry, "Remarks with Brazilian Foreign Minister Antonio de Aguiar Patriota After Their Meeting," Itamaraty Palace, Brasilia, Brazil, August 13, 2013.

[17] Tovah Lazaroff, "272 West Bank settler homes approved, settlement of Ofra gets 'master plan,'" *jpost.com*, January 7, 2014.

[18] Avi Issacharoff, "Hamas, circa 2013, is in a lot of trouble," *Times of Israel*, October 29, 2013.

Figure 1. Map of West Bank

PA Governorates; Areas A, B, and C; and Selected Israeli Settlements

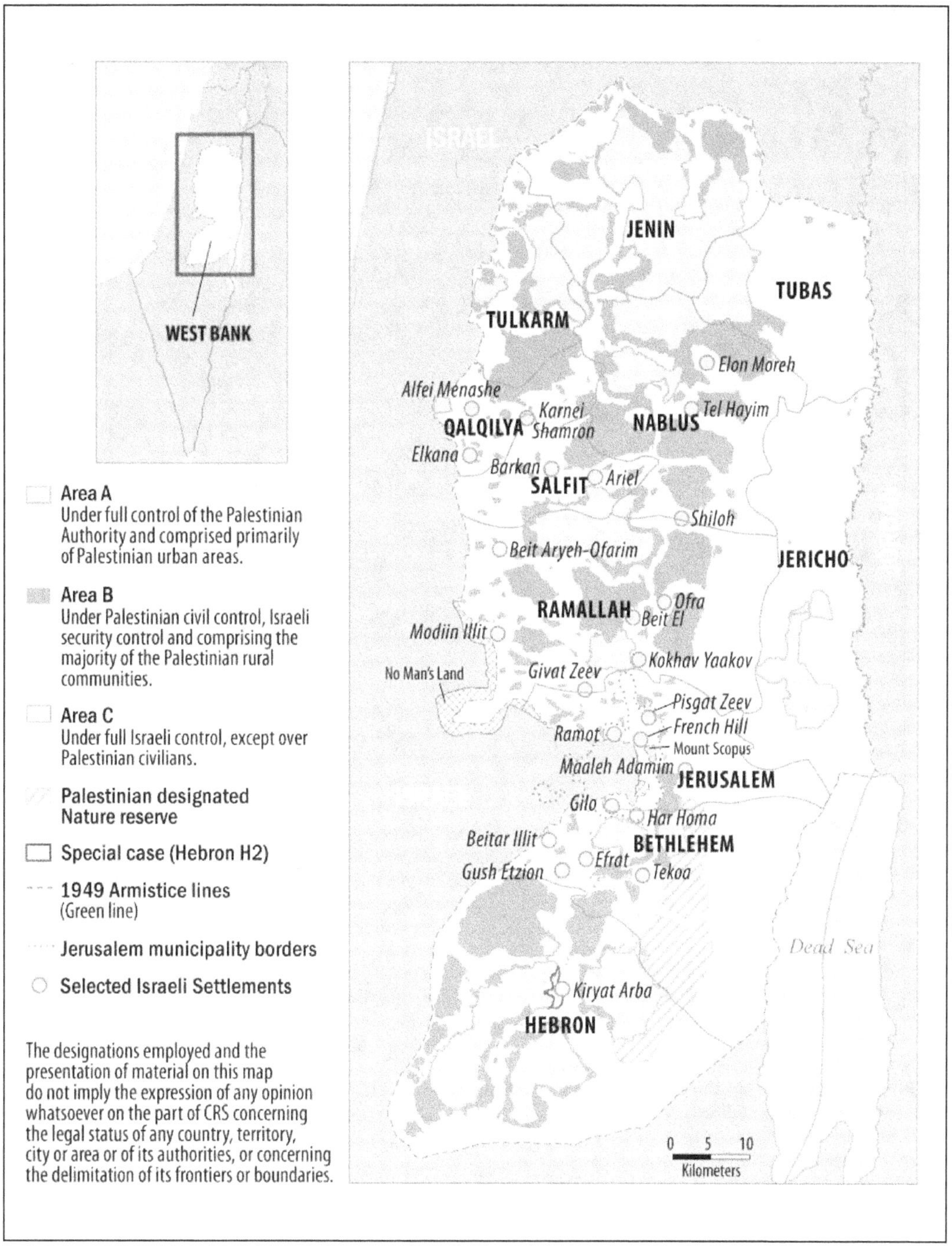

Source: CRS, adapted from the U.N. Office for the Coordination of Humanitarian Affairs.

Notes: All boundaries and depictions are approximate. Israeli settlements are not drawn to scale and do not reflect the full scope of Jewish residential construction in the West Bank and East Jerusalem. Areas A, B, and C were designated pursuant to the Israeli-Palestinian Interim Agreement on the West Bank and the Gaza Strip, dated September 28, 1995. H2 was designated pursuant to the Protocol Concerning the Redeployment in Hebron, dated January 17, 1997. Additional Israeli settlements exist within Area C but are not denoted, particularly a group of settlements with small populations located along the Jordanian border (the Jordan Valley).

Figure 2. Map of Gaza Strip

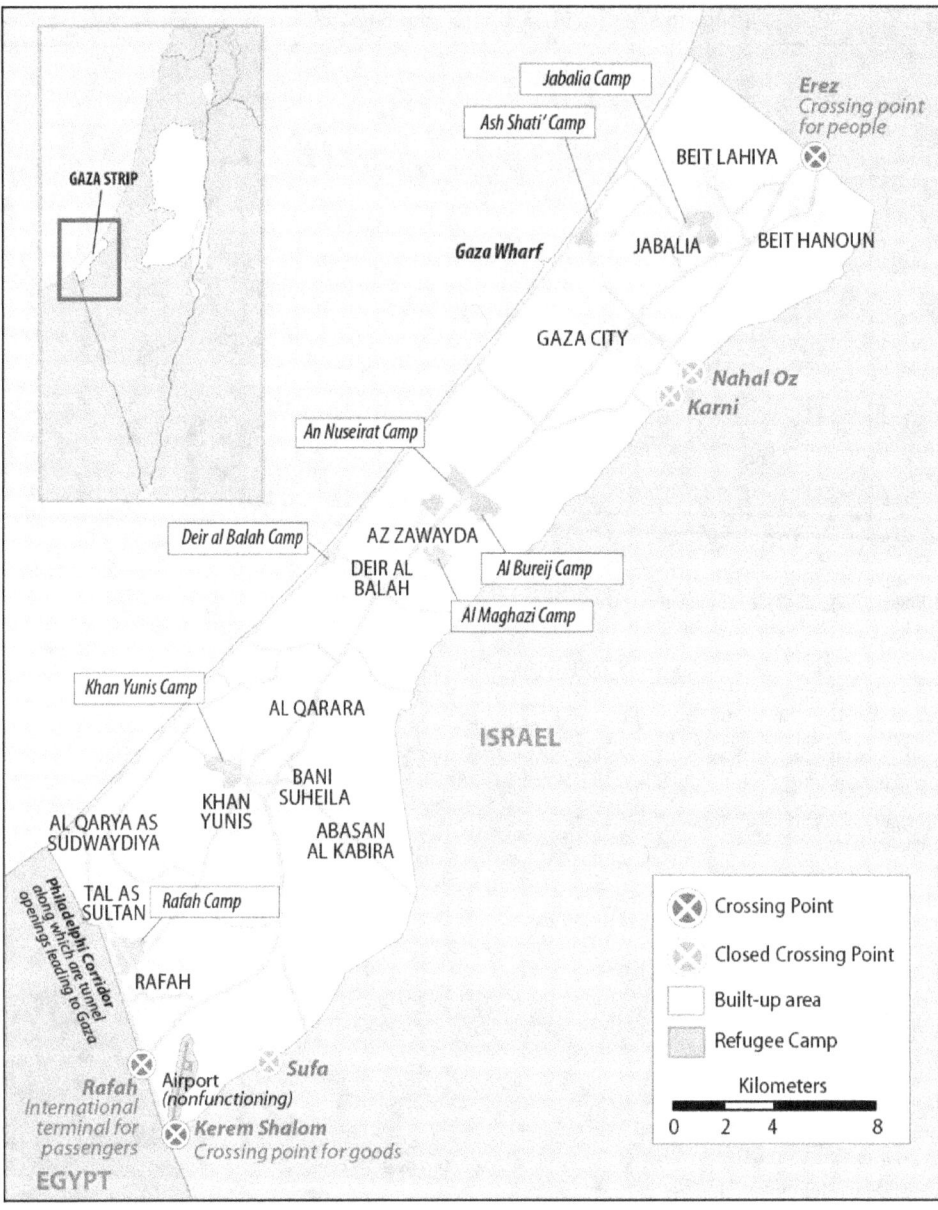

Source: U.N. Office for the Coordination of Humanitarian Affairs and UNOSAT, with additional data from UNRWA; adapted by CRS.

Demographic and Economic Profile

There are an estimated 4.48 million Palestinians living in the West Bank, Gaza Strip, and East Jerusalem (approximately 2.75 million in the West Bank and East Jerusalem, and 1.73 million in Gaza).[19] Of these, approximately 2 million are registered as refugees (in their own right or as descendants of the original refugees) from the 1947-1948 Arab-Israeli war. (In addition,

---

[19] Palestinian Central Bureau of Statistics (PCBS), 2013. PCBS also reports that an additional 1.4 million Palestinians live as Arab citizens of Israel.

approximately 500,000 Jewish Israeli citizens live in the West Bank and East Jerusalem.) Another some 3 million Palestinians live as refugees in Jordan, Lebanon, and Syria, in addition to non-refugees living in these states and elsewhere around the world.

Table 1. Estimated Palestinian Population Worldwide

Country or Region	Population
West Bank, Gaza Strip, and East Jerusalem	4,476,000
Israel	1,430,000
Arab states	5,226,000
Other states	665,000
Total	**11,797,000**

Source: Palestinian Central Bureau of Statistics, 2013.

West Bank Palestinians generally are wealthier, better educated, and more secular than their Gazan counterparts. The Palestinian population in the West Bank and Gaza has one of the highest growth rates in the world and is disproportionately young. According to the Palestinian Central Bureau of Statistics, 39.9% of the Palestinians in the territories as of 2013 were less than 15 years old. The youth bulge ensures that the population growth rate will remain high even as fertility rates decline. Possible implications were summarized thusly in a March 2009 Brookings Institution report:

> If young people are engaged in productive roles, the Palestinian youth bulge can be a positive factor in economic development. Human capital is the main comparative advantage that Palestinian Territories have over naturally resource-rich countries in the Middle East. Yet, as in any economy, a large cohort of young Palestinians will continue to exert pressure on the education system and labor markets.[20]

Palestinians are well educated relative to other Arab countries, with an adult literacy rate of 95%. (Jordan and Egypt, by comparison, have a 92% and a 66% adult literacy rate, respectively.)[21] The Palestinian population in the West Bank and Gaza is approximately 98% Sunni Muslim; approximately 1% is Christian of various denominations.[22]

Table 2. Basic Facts for the West Bank and Gaza Strip

Statistic	West Bank	Gaza Strip	Combined
Population (2013 est.)	2,746,000	1,730,000	4,476,000
Refugees (2014 est.)	741,000	1,203,000	1,944,000
Median age (2013 est.)	22.0	18.1	-

---

[20] Nawtej Dhillon, "Beyond Reconstruction: What Lies Ahead for Young Palestinians," Brookings Institution, March 2009.

[21] United Nations Children's Fund (UNICEF) data, available at http://www.childinfo.org/education_literacy.php.

[22] State Department International Religious Freedom Report for 2012.

Statistic	West Bank	Gaza Strip	Combined
Population growth rate (2013 est.)	2.0%	3.0%	-
GDP growth rate (2013 est.)	-0.6% (Q1)	12.0% (Q1)	3.5%
GDP per capita (purchasing power parity) (2008 est.)	-	-	$2,900
Unemployment rate (2013 est.)	18.6%	29.5%	22.3%
Inflation rate (2011 est.)	-	-	1.7%
Population below poverty line (2011 est.)	17.8%	38.8%	-
Exports (2011 est.)	-	-	$846.1 mil
Export commodities	stone, olives, fruit, vegetables	citrus, flowers, textiles	-
Export partners (2010 est.)	-	-	Israel 84.5%, Arab states 11.4%, Europe 1.7%
Imports (2010 est.)			$5.5 bil
Import commodities	food, consumer goods, construction materials, petroleum, chemicals	food, consumer goods	-
Import partners (2010 est.)	-	-	Israel 72.6%, Asia 11.6%, Europe 9.8%

Sources: Central Intelligence Agency, Palestinian Central Bureau of Statistics, World Bank, *Economist Intelligence Unit*, UNRWA.

Sources: Population figures exclude Israeli settlers.

The Regional and International Context

In General

Without sovereignty or a self-sufficient economy, Palestinians' fortunes depend to a large degree on the policies of other countries and international organizations with influence in the surrounding region. Almost every aspect of Palestinian existence has some connection with Israel given Israel's occupation of the West Bank; its effective unilateral annexation of East Jerusalem; and its large measure of control over borders, resources, and trade in both the West Bank and Gaza. Both Israelis and Palestinians continue to acknowledge that the United States helps define both regional and international frameworks within which they and other international actors address their mutual issues. Some observers believe that the Israeli-Palestinian conflict commands less U.S. attention than it deserves because issues in other areas of the region and world distract attention from it. Others suggest that U.S. involvement with and support to the Palestinians demonstrates that the United States does accord the conflict priority status despite many other existing global concerns.

Some observers argue that Arab states have been historically complicit in prolonging the plight of the Palestinians (and Palestinian refugees in particular) because doing so pressures Israel and serves Arab states' domestic interests by deflecting attention from domestic problems and by avoiding difficulties that might result from assimilating the refugees into their societies. It is unclear what effect ongoing political change in Arab states will have on the Palestinian question and its various Israeli and Palestinian stakeholders. Potential effects of political change could include intensified jockeying by powers such as Iran, Turkey, and Saudi Arabia to use the Palestinian issue for regional influence, or further destabilization and use of neighboring territory by criminal or terrorist networks in Syria, Lebanon, and Egypt's Sinai Peninsula.

International Recognition of Palestinian Statehood and U.N. Initiatives

Some 130 out of 193 U.N. member states have reportedly formally recognized the state of Palestine that was declared by the PLO in 1988, but none yet among the North American and Western European countries that are the PA's main financial patrons and exercise considerable political influence in the region.

On November 29, 2012, the U.N. General Assembly (UNGA) adopted Resolution 67/19 by a vote of 138 member states in favor (including 14 European Union countries—France and Spain among them), 9 against (including the United States and Israel), and 41 abstentions. The resolution changed the permanent U.N. observer status of the PLO (recognized as "Palestine" within the U.N. system) from an "entity" to a "non-member state." The change in observer status effected by Resolution 67/19 is largely symbolic.[23] At the same time, this change might increase the probability that the Palestinians and other international actors could take steps—particularly in the International Criminal Court (ICC)—to make legal action possible against perceived Israeli violations of various international laws and norms regarding the treatment of people and property in the West Bank and Gaza.[24]

The adoption of Resolution 67/19 was part of the broader PLO effort to obtain greater international recognition of Palestinian statehood, possibly intended to strengthen the PLO's hand in negotiations. The United States and Israel are concerned that additional or renewed Palestinian recourse to international forums could circumvent—and thus undermine—U.S.-mediated negotiations or stoke popular unrest. In September 2011, PLO Chairman Abbas applied for

---

[23] The PLO has had permanent observer status at the United Nations since 1974. Following the adoption of Resolution 67/19, "Palestine" maintains many of the capacities it had as an observer entity—including participation in General Assembly debates and the ability to co-sponsor draft resolutions and decisions related to proceedings on Palestinian and Middle East issues. Despite its new designation as a "state," "Palestine" is not a member of the United Nations, and therefore does not have the right to vote or to call for a vote in the General Assembly on resolutions. However, in November 2013, the "State of Palestine" participated in the balloting for a judge for the International Tribunal for the Former Yugoslavia. Article 13, Section 2(d) of the Statute for the Tribunal (Annex to U.N. Doc. S/25704, adopted pursuant to U.N. Security Council Resolution 827 (1993), as subsequently amended) includes "non-Member States maintaining permanent observer missions at United Nations Headquarters" in the election of the tribunal's judges.

[24] An April 2012 opinion by the ICC's Office of the Prosecutor, which determined that there was no basis for it to consider a declaration of consent by "Palestine" to ICC jurisdiction in the West Bank and Gaza, appeared to rule that guidance from the UNGA would be decisive in determining whether the PLO or PA had competence as a state to consent to ICC jurisdiction. International Criminal Court, Office of the Prosecutor, "Situation in Palestine," April 3, 2012. One analysis asserts, however, that legal ambiguities remain. John Cerone, "Legal Implications of the UN General Assembly Vote to Accord Palestine the Status of Observer State," *insights*, American Society of International Law, December 7, 2012. For more information on the ICC, see CRS Report R41116, *The International Criminal Court (ICC): Jurisdiction, Extradition, and U.S. Policy*, by Matthew C. Weed.

Palestinian membership in the United Nations. The application remains pending in the Security Council's membership committee, whose members did not achieve consensus during 2011 deliberations.[25] The application for Palestinian membership would likely face a U.S. veto if it came to a future vote in the Security Council.

In the fall of 2011, the Palestinians did obtain membership in the U.N. Educational, Scientific and Cultural Organization (UNESCO).[26] They appear to be using their UNESCO membership to establish and advance claims of Palestinian "self-determination and cultural rights"[27] over sites such as the Church of the Nativity in Bethlehem. In June 2012, UNESCO inscribed (designated) the church as both a World Heritage Site and a World Heritage Site in Danger.[28]

Under U.S. laws passed in 1990 and 1994,[29] Palestinian admission to membership in UNESCO in 2011 triggered the withholding of U.S. assessed and voluntary financial contributions to the organization.[30] If the Palestinians were to obtain membership in other U.N. entities, the 1990 and 1994 U.S. laws might trigger withholdings of U.S. financial contributions to these entities. Such withholdings could adversely affect these entities' budgets and complicate the conduct of U.S. foreign policy within the U.N. system and other multilateral settings.

---

[25] United Nations Security Council, "Report of the Committee on the Admission of New Members concerning the application of Palestine for admission to membership in the United Nations," S/2011/705, November 11, 2011. Paragraph 19 of this report provides a summary of the varying views that committee members advanced regarding Palestinian membership: "The view was expressed that the Committee should recommend to the Council that Palestine be admitted to membership in the United Nations. A different view was expressed that the membership application could not be supported at this time and an abstention was envisaged in the event of a vote. Yet another view expressed was that there were serious questions about the application, that the applicant did not meet the requirements for membership and that a favourable recommendation to the General Assembly would not be supported."

[26] For more information, see CRS Report R42999, *The United Nations Educational, Scientific, and Cultural Organization (UNESCO)*, by Luisa Blanchfield and Marjorie Ann Browne.

[27] Isabel Kershner, "UNESCO Adds Nativity Church in Bethlehem to Heritage List," *New York Times*, June 29, 2012.

[28] Inclusion on the World Heritage List means that a site should be protected and preserved by the global community; inclusion on the Danger List means that a site is particularly threatened. In response to the designations, David Killion, U.S. Ambassador to UNESCO, stated that the Danger List is generally reserved only "for extreme cases, such as when a site is under imminent threat of destruction." Killion also noted that in the past 40 years, only four other sites had been added to the Danger List. Statement by Ambassador Killion on the Emergency Inscription of the Church of the Nativity as a World Heritage Site, U.S. Mission to UNESCO, June 29, 2012.

[29] P.L. 101-246 (Foreign Relations Authorization Act, Fiscal Years 1990 and 1991) and P.L. 103-236 (Foreign Relations Authorization Act, Fiscal Years 1994 and 1995).

[30] In the Obama Administration's FY2014 budget request, it stated that it "seeks Congressional support for legislation that would provide authority to waive" these legislative restrictions. FY2014 State Department Congressional Budget Justification, Volume 1: Department of State Operations, p. 494. If Members of Congress sought to lift or modify these restrictions, they could amend the applicable legal provisions or propose stand-alone legislation. A version of the Department of State, Foreign Operations, and Related Programs Appropriations Act, Fiscal Year 2014 (S. 1372) reported favorably by the Senate Appropriations Committee included a provision that would have permitted the executive branch to make contributions to UNESCO's World Heritage Fund, but this provision was not included in the Consolidated Appropriations Act, 2014 (P.L. 113-76). Senator Mary Landrieu authored this provision and sought support for it from the leadership of the Appropriations Committees in a letter dated December 18, 2013. The text of the letter is available at http://www.landrieu.senate.gov/files/documents/2013_12_18_SFOPS_Appropriations_Conference_Letter.pdf.

Matters of General Congressional Interest

U.S. and International Assistance to the Palestinians

Overview

See CRS Report RS22967, *U.S. Foreign Aid to the Palestinians*, by Jim Zanotti, for a more detailed description of this topic and the particulars of U.S. assistance, the various conditions to which it is subject, and recent informal congressional holds. The PA's dependence on foreign assistance is acute—largely a result of the distortion of the West Bank/Gaza economy in the 47 years since Israeli occupation began and the bloat of the PA's payroll since its inception about 20 years ago. Facing a regular annual budget deficit of over $1 billion, PA officials regularly seek aid from the United States and other international sources to meet the PA's financial commitments. Absent major structural changes in revenue and expenses, which do not appear likely in the near term despite some ambitious PA goals and projections, this dependence will likely continue. The effectiveness of U.S. assistance to the Palestinians in furthering U.S. policy objectives is challenged, logistically and strategically, by the shifting and often conflicting interests of Israel, the PLO, the PA, Fatah, and Hamas. Effectiveness is also challenged by the U.S. interagency process, as well as the need to coordinate activities and assistance with other donor states and with international organizations and coordinating mechanisms such as the European Union, United Nations,[31] World Bank, the Office of the Quartet Representative, and the Ad Hoc Liaison Committee,[32] among others.

Palestinian International Initiatives: Effect on U.S. Aid

The Palestinians have faced reprisals from the United States and Israel for their initiatives in the United Nations system, including informal Congressional holds that delayed disbursement of FY2011 and FY2012 U.S. aid and temporary Israeli unwillingness to transfer tax and customs revenues due the PA.[33] The United States and Israel may be reluctant to adopt drastic or permanent measures because of concerns regarding the PA's financial fragility and a lack of Israeli appetite for stepping in to fill the void or calm the disorder that could result from undermining the self-rule institutions of West Bank Palestinians.

In the event that the PLO's status in the United Nations or any U.N. specialized agency other than UNESCO approaches the level of membership, two separate provisions from Section 7041(j)(2) of the Consolidated Appropriations Act, 2014 (P.L. 113-76) could be triggered. The first, which is subject to a waiver by the Secretary of State for national security reasons, would prevent Economic Support Fund aid (ESF) from going to the PA. The second could prohibit the President

---

[31] Over the years, U.N. organs have set up a number of bodies or offices, as well as five U.N. peacekeeping operations, which have or had mandates or functions directly related to Palestine or the Arab-Israeli dispute.

[32] The Ad Hoc Liaison Committee is a coordinating mechanism for Israel, the PA, and all major international actors providing assistance to the Palestinians that was established in the mid-1990s to facilitate reform and development in the West Bank and Gaza in connection with the Oslo process. Norway permanently chairs the committee, which meets periodically in various international venues and is divided into sectors with their own heads for discrete issue areas such as economic development, security and justice, and civil society.

[33] CRS Report RS22967, *U.S. Foreign Aid to the Palestinians*, by Jim Zanotti.

from permitting the PLO to maintain its representative office in Washington, DC. Every six months since the early days of the peace process in the mid-1990s, each successive President has waived a 1987 legal prohibition against the existence of a PLO representative office.[34]

These two provisions of Section 7041(j)(2) would be triggered if the Palestinians obtain "the same standing as member states or full membership as a state outside an agreement negotiated between Israel and the Palestinians" in the United Nations or any U.N. specialized agency other than UNESCO. If the second provision is triggered, a presidential waiver would only be eligible—after an additional 90 days—if the President certifies to Congress that the Palestinians have entered into "direct and meaningful negotiations with Israel." The first provision in Section 7041(j)(2) preventing ESF from going to the PA (subject to waiver for national security reasons by the Secretary of State) would also be triggered if Palestinians "initiate an International Criminal Court judicially authorized investigation, or actively support such an investigation, that subjects Israeli nationals to an investigation for alleged crimes against Palestinians."

Terrorism and Militancy

Hamas and Other Groups: Background and Methods

Hamas (see **Appendix A** and **Appendix B** for an overview of the organization and its key leaders) and seven other Palestinian groups have been designated Foreign Terrorist Organizations (FTOs) by the State Department: Abu Nidal Organization, Al Aqsa Martyrs' Brigades, Army of Islam, Palestine Liberation Front – Abu Abbas Faction, Palestine Islamic Jihad – Shaqaqi Faction, Popular Front for the Liberation of Palestine, and Popular Front for the Liberation of Palestine-General Command. Most Palestinian militant groups claim that they are opposed to peace with Israel on principle, but some—such as the Fatah-affiliated Al Aqsa Martyrs' Brigades—view militancy and terror as tactics that can be used to improve the Palestinians' negotiating position. Since Oslo in 1993, these groups have engaged in a variety of methods of violence, killing approximately 1,350 Israelis (over 900 civilians—including Jewish settlers in the Palestinian territories—and 450 security force personnel).[35] Palestinians who insist that they are engaging in asymmetric warfare with a stronger enemy point to the approximately 7,000 deaths inflicted on Palestinians by Israelis since 1993,[36] some through acts of terrorism aimed at civilians.[37]

Although damage is difficult to measure qualitatively, suicide bombings have constituted a fearsome means of attack, claiming approximately 700 Israeli lives (mostly civilians within Israel proper).[38] After peaking during the second intifada years of 2001-2003, suicide bombings have

---

[34] Anti-Terrorism Act of 1987 (P.L. 100-204, §1003).

[35] Statistics culled from B'Tselem (The Israeli Information Center for Human Rights in the Occupied Territories) website at http://www.btselem.org/statistics.

[36] Ibid.

[37] The most prominent attack by an Israeli civilian against Palestinians since 1993 was the killing of at least 29 Palestinians (and possibly between 10 to 23 more) and the wounding of about 150 more by Israeli settler Baruch Goldstein (a Brooklyn-born former military doctor) at the Ibrahimi Mosque (Mosque of Abraham) in the Cave of the Patriarchs in Hebron on February 25, 1994 (the Jewish holy day of Purim) while the victims were at prayer. See George J. Church, "When Fury Rules," *Time*, March 7, 1994. This incident has been cited by many analysts as a provocation for the Palestinian suicide bombing campaign that followed.

[38] Suicide bombing figures culled from Israel Ministry of Foreign Affairs website at http://www.mfa.gov.il/MFA/Terrorism-+Obstacle+to+Peace/Palestinian+terror+before+2000/
(continued...)

---

largely ceased (two occurrences and four deaths since early 2006). Many observers attribute the drop-off to enhanced Israeli security measures—the Israeli military's withdrawal from Gaza in 2005 and the general closure of its borders, the West Bank separation barrier, and tightening of border checkpoints. Additionally, some analysts have posited, as contributing factors, Hamas's entry into a position of responsibility and political power, the strengthening of PA security forces in the West Bank, and general Palestinian exhaustion with violence.

Isolated attacks still occur within Israel and the West Bank, often perpetrated by Palestinians using small arms or vehicles as weapons. Militants also stage attacks and attempt to capture Israeli soldiers, including at or near Gaza border crossings, and since 2011 have engaged in a few instances of cross-border attack from redoubts within Egypt's Sinai Peninsula—an international border less vulnerable to Israeli reprisals. Antipathy between Jewish settlers and Palestinian residents in the West Bank leads to occasional attacks and acts of vandalism on both sides— particularly in Hebron and in the northern West Bank near Nablus.

The most pronounced trend since Israel's disengagement from Gaza in 2005 has been an increased firing of rockets and mortars from the territory, now controlled by Hamas. The over 10,000 rockets, mortars, and anti-tank missiles fired by Palestinians since 2001 have killed approximately 30 Israelis and wounded hundreds.[39] The persistent threat of rocket fire has had a broader negative psychological effect on Israelis living in targeted communities.[40] Because rockets are fired indiscriminately without regard for avoiding these communities, most neutral observers characterize this as tantamount to intentional targeting of civilians.

Over the past decade-plus, tunnels leading from Egypt's Sinai Peninsula into Gaza have allowed militants to smuggle raw materials used to make crude, short-range explosives (commonly known as "Qassam rockets"). In more recent years, pre-manufactured Grad-style and Fajr rockets (thought to come from Iran) with ranges of up to 45 miles have also been smuggled into Gaza. During a weeklong conflict in November 2012 involving Palestinian militants and Israel, Iranian Revolutionary Guard Corps (IRGC) commander General Mohammed Ali Jafari was quoted as saying that Iran was transferring weapons technology to Palestinians in Gaza so that they could build "an unlimited number of these missiles."[41] These rockets, known as M-75s, have reported ranges similar to Fajrs,[42] apparently relieving Palestinian militants' dependence on smuggling to refresh their arsenals.

(...continued)

Suicide%20and%20Other%20Bombing%20Attacks%20in%20Israel%20Since.

[39] http://www.btselem.org/statistics; "Rocket Threat to Israel: Palestinian Rocket & Mortar Attacks (February 2009-Present)," Jewish Virtual Library; "Q&A: Gaza conflict," *BBC News*, January 18, 2009.

[40] Toni O'Loughlin and Hazem Balousha, "News: Air Strikes on Gaza," *The Observer* (UK), December 28, 2008; David Isby, "Effective Anti-Qassam Defence Could Be More Than Six Years Away," *Jane's Missiles and Rockets*, January 1, 2007.

[41] Thomas Erdbrink, "Iranian Missiles in Gaza Fight Give Tehran Government a Lift," *New York Times*, November 21, 2012.

[42] Adiv Sterman, "Palestinians in Gaza said to test long-range rocket," *Times of Israel*, December 31, 2013.

Figure 3. Possible Ranges of Rockets and Missiles from Palestinian Militant Groups and Hezbollah

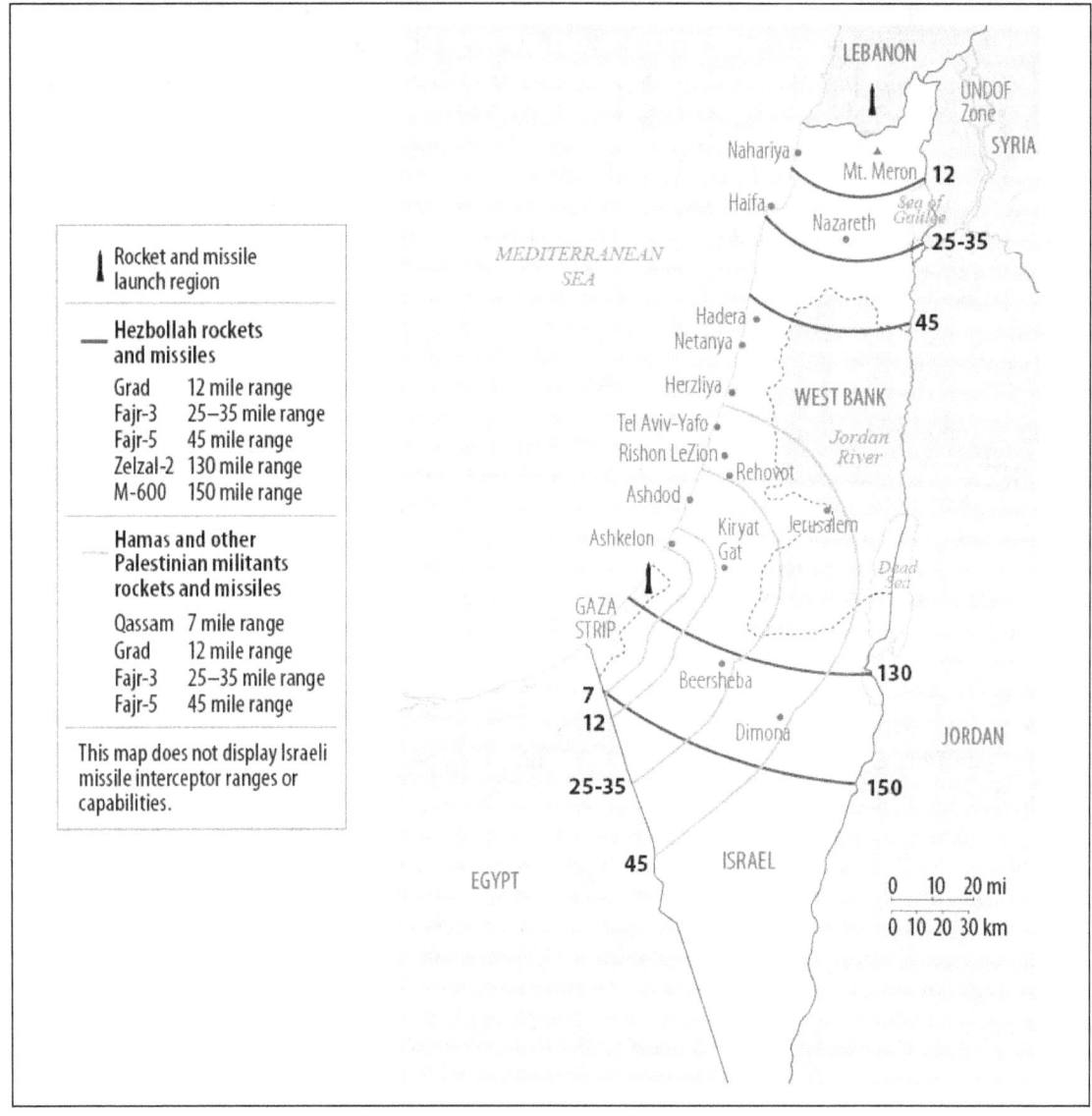

Source: Bipartisan Policy Center, February 2012, adapted by CRS.

Note: All ranges are approximate.

Addressing Continuing Threats

Sporadic instances of Israeli-Palestinian violence and unrest in the West Bank have increased in frequency since late 2013, leading to some speculation about the potential for a new intifada. However, a December 2013 article stated that "Israeli army intelligence officers and Palestinian analysts say the latest bloodshed is markedly different from the violence that defined the intifadas, or uprisings, of the late 1980s and early 2000s…. [T]he violence by Palestinians in the West Bank appears to be more intimate and less sophisticated; more spontaneous than organized;

and carried out, for the most part, without any apparent backing by militant or political organizations."[43] On Israeli television in November 2012, Abbas said, "As long as I am here in this office there will be no armed third intifada. Never. We don't want to use terror. We don't want to use force. We don't want to use weapons."[44] Nevertheless, reports continue regarding militant organizations and terrorist cells operating in the West Bank (including East Jerusalem), including some focusing on targets within Israel proper. In January 2014, one report alleged that Israel had arrested three Palestinians from East Jerusalem who had been recruited online to carry out multiple bombings—including the U.S. embassy in Tel Aviv—by an Al Qaeda operative in Gaza.[45]

In addition to developing and deploying the Iron Dome anti-rocket system,[46] Israel also continually seeks U.S. and international help to slow or stop the Gaza smuggling network. These concerns have been heightened by the periodic attacks from Palestinians based in Sinai, including occasional rocket fire aimed at the Israeli Red Sea port of Eilat. However, reports indicate that the Egyptian military has significantly disrupted the use of Gaza-Sinai tunnels since it ousted Muhammad Morsi as president in July 2013.

Israeli authorities express concern that Palestinian militants might soon acquire longer-range rockets and precision targeting capabilities that would increase the danger to larger population centers such as Tel Aviv. The possibility that a more dangerous rocket threat could emerge in the West Bank—especially in light of Iran's apparent transfer of weapons production know-how to Palestinian militants based in Gaza—is one factor underlying Israeli reluctance to consider withdrawal without copious security guarantees. The possibility also exists of a coordinated or simultaneous rocket attack by Palestinian militants from Gaza and by the militant, Iran-supported Lebanese Shiite group Hezbollah.

Palestinian Governance

Achieving effective and transparent governance over the West Bank and Gaza and preventing Israeli-Palestinian violence, while facing a continued Israeli settler and military presence, has proven elusive since the limited self-rule experiment began in 1994. Many observers say that the task became even more difficult following the split established in 2007 between a Fatah-led PA in the West Bank and a de facto Hamas regime in Gaza.

Palestinian Authority (PA)

The Palestinian National Authority (or Palestinian Authority, hereinafter PA) was granted limited rule (under supervening Israeli occupational authority) in the Gaza Strip and parts of the West Bank in the mid-1990s pursuant to the Oslo Accords.[47] Although not a state, the PA is organized

---

[43] William Booth and Ruth Eglash, "West Bank violence jumps, but this time it's more personal," *Washington Post*, December 1, 2013.

[44] Transcript of Israel Channel 2 interview with Mahmoud Abbas in Ramallah, West Bank, November 1, 2012, Open Source Center GMP20121102746002.

[45] Yaakov Lappin, "3 east Jerusalem al-Qaida recruits arrested, 'planned massive bombings,'" *jpost.com*, January 22, 2014.

[46] For more information on Iron Dome, see CRS Report RL33476, *Israel: Background and U.S. Relations*, by Jim Zanotti; and CRS Report RL33222, *U.S. Foreign Aid to Israel*, by Jeremy M. Sharp.

[47] The relevant Israel-PLO agreements that created the PA and established its parameters were the Agreement on the (continued...)

---

like one—complete with democratic mechanisms; security forces; and executive, legislative, and judicial organs of governance. Ramallah is its de facto seat, but is not considered to be the PA capital because of Palestinian determination to make Jerusalem (or at least the part east of the 1967 lines) the capital of a Palestinian state. The executive branch has both a president and a prime minister-led cabinet, the Palestinian Legislative Council (PLC) is its legislature, and the judicial branch has separate high courts to decide substantive disputes and to settle constitutional controversies, as well as a High Judicial Council.[48] The electoral base of the PA is composed of Palestinians from the West Bank, Jerusalem, and the Gaza Strip.

After Hamas won January 2006 PLC elections, a factional standoff between Fatah and Hamas ensued—with Abbas as PA president and Hamas controlling the PLC and the government ministries.[49] These tensions ultimately led to armed conflict that led to Hamas's forcible takeover of the Gaza Strip in June 2007. In response to the Hamas takeover, PA President Abbas dissolved the Hamas-led government and appointed a "caretaker" technocratic PA government in the West Bank.

The PLC is currently sidelined due to its lack of a quorum caused by the West Bank/Gaza split. However, Hamas uses its 2006 electoral mandate as an argument—along with the argument that Abbas used extra-legal means to dismiss its government—to legitimize its rule over Gaza.

Because some PA leaders hold overlapping leadership roles within the PLO and various factions, it is difficult to gauge the degree to which Palestinians consider the PA truly authoritative or legitimate even within the West Bank. For example, until his death in 2004, Yasser Arafat served as PA president, PLO chairman, and head of Fatah, and following Arafat's death, Mahmoud Abbas has succeeded him in each of these roles. Many observers wonder how the PLO and PA will coordinate their functions and be regarded by the Palestinian people at a future point when the leadership of the two institutions and of Fatah might be different. It is possible that the PA could somehow forge an identity completely independent from (and perhaps in competition with) the PLO. Alternatively, the PLO might attempt to restructure or dissolve the PA (either in concert with Israel or unilaterally) pursuant to the claim that the PA is a constitutional creature of PLO agreements with Israel.[50]

Prospects for Economic Self-Sufficiency

Lacking a self-sufficient private sector, the Palestinians' economic prospects have historically depended on easy entry into and exit out of Israel for their workers and goods. Yet, following the

---

(...continued)

Gaza Strip and the Jericho Area, dated May 4, 1994; and the Israeli-Palestinian Interim Agreement on the West Bank and the Gaza Strip, dated September 28, 1995.

[48] See U.N. Development Programme—Programme on Governance in the Arab Region website at http://www.pogar.org/countries/country.aspx?cid=14. However, human rights groups have voiced concern that the PA executive continues to circumvent civilian courts that might check its power by employing military courts on a wider range of matters than the civilian courts deem proper. See The Goldstone Report, dated September 25, 2009, pp. 337-338, available at http://www2.ohchr.org/english/bodies/hrcouncil/specialsession/9/FactFindingMission.htm.

[49] This time, the United States and Israel supported increasing the power of the PA presidency at the expense of the Hamas prime minister and cabinet—a turnabout from their 2003 approach to the organs of PA governance when Arafat was PA president.

[50] The PA was originally intended to be a temporary, transitional mechanism for the five-year period prescribed for final-status negotiations, not an indefinite administrative authority.

outbreak of the second intifada in 2000, this access largely ceased. Israel constructed a West Bank separation barrier and increased security at crossing points. It now issues permits to control access, and periodically halts the flow of people and goods altogether. Alternatives to Palestinian economic interdependence with Israel would likely be

- to attract investment and build a self-sufficient economy, which is probably years if not decades away;

- to look to neighboring Egypt and Jordan (which struggle with their own political and economic problems) for economic integration; or

- to depend indefinitely upon external assistance.

For the West Bank and Gaza to attract enough long-term investment to become self-sufficient, most observers agree that uncertainties regarding the political and security situation and Israeli movement restrictions would need to be significantly reduced or eliminated.[51] The PA routinely faces crises in finding budgetary funds from donors or lending sources, occasionally even receiving emergency advances from Israel on the tax and custom revenues it regularly collects on the PA's behalf.

In the wake of Israel's tapping of natural gas fields off its coast, reports as of January 2014 indicate that the PA is discussing the prospect of developing the Marine gas field discovered off Gaza's coast in 2000 with the British company that controls the rights to the field.[52] Reports also indicate that the PA might be discussing a deal with Russia to exploit gas off the Gaza coast and possibly oil in the West Bank.[53] Additionally, the PA has supposedly agreed with the companies developing Israel's Leviathan offshore gas field to export gas that would power a new generation plant in the northern West Bank when Leviathan comes online in coming years.[54] PA cooperation with Israel on energy may extend to water resources as well, given the PA's agreement in December 2013 with Israel and Jordan on a plan to pursue a version of the Red Sea-Dead Sea canal that would provide discounted freshwater to Palestinians.[55]

West Bank: Fatah and Israel

The Fatah-led Palestinian Authority administers densely populated Palestinian areas in the West Bank subject to supervening Israeli control under the Oslo agreements (see **Figure 1** above for map).[56] Israel Defense Forces (IDF) soldiers regularly mount arrest operations to apprehend wanted Palestinians or foil terrorist plots, and maintain permanent posts throughout the West Bank and along the West Bank's administrative borders with Israel and Jordan to protect Jewish settlers and broader security interests.

---

[51] See, e.g., World Bank, *Economic Monitoring Report to the Ad Hoc Liaison Committee*, September 25, 2013.

[52] Gwen Ackerman and Riad Hamade, "Palestinians Pin Hopes on Gas Project to Counter Donor Fatigue," *Bloomberg News*, January 28, 2014.

[53] Yifa Yaakov, "Abbas, Medvedev negotiating $1b. Gaza gas deal," *Times of Israel*, January 25, 2014.

[54] "Leviathan Partners Sign Deal with Palestinians," *Oil Daily*, January 7, 2014.

[55] For more details, see CRS Report RL33546, *Jordan: Background and U.S. Relations*, by Jeremy M. Sharp.

[56] The two agreements that define respective Israeli and PA zones of control are (1) the Israeli-Palestinian Interim Agreement on the West Bank and the Gaza Strip, dated September 28, 1995; and (2) the Protocol Concerning the Redeployment in Hebron, dated January 17, 1997. East Jerusalem is excluded from these agreements, as Israel has effectively annexed it.

Coordination between Israeli and PA authorities generally takes place on a case-by-case basis and usually discreetly, given the political sensitivity for PA leaders to be seen "collaborating" with Israeli occupiers. The physical and psychological effects of Operation Defensive Shield linger. During the operation, which took place in early 2002 at the height of the second intifada, Israel reoccupied PA-controlled areas of the West Bank—demolishing many official PA buildings, Palestinian neighborhoods, and other infrastructure; and reinforcing many Palestinians' opinion that Israel retained ultimate control over their lives.

Many observers note signs of progress with PA security capacities and West Bank economic development since 2007, along with greater Israeli cooperation. It is less clear whether the progress they cite can be made self-sustaining and can be useful in promoting a broader political solution.[57] Some analysts are concerned that, without a functioning Palestinian legislature and with the prospect of future PA elections uncertain, the rule of President Abbas is becoming less legitimate and more authoritarian and corrupt. This could complicate the process of political succession whenever Abbas leaves office. Many analysts interpret the April 2013 resignation of Salam Fayyad—a Western-friendly figure—as PA prime minister, and Abbas's June 2013 appointment of political neophyte Rami Hamdallah to replace Fayyad, as a consolidation of Abbas's power.[58] Some commentators have expressed concern that Fayyad's departure will damage efforts to promote the "new source of legitimacy" they say he introduced to the Palestinian national narrative—one based on internal reform and development, "not on a legacy of resistance or on religion."[59]

Gaza: Hamas, Israel, and Egypt (Sinai)[60]

After victory in the 2006 PA legislative elections, internal Hamas political and military leaders in the West Bank and Gaza gained greater power, and then consolidated this power in Gaza—while losing it in the West Bank—through violent struggle with Fatah in June 2007. Still claiming a leadership role within the PA due to its electoral mandate, Hamas has maintained power in Gaza ever since—even following a three-week conflict with Israel in December 2008 and January 2009 (code-named "Operation Cast Lead" by Israel) that significantly damaged the territory's infrastructure. The quiet following Cast Lead allowed Hamas to rearm through Gaza's smuggling network—with much of its money, weapons, and other supplies reportedly originating in Iran.[61] See **Figure 2** above for a map of Gaza.

---

[57] For a more detailed discussion of the issues raised in this paragraph, see CRS Report RS22967, *U.S. Foreign Aid to the Palestinians*, by Jim Zanotti.

[58] Abbas simultaneously appointed or re-appointed some of his close associates to other key cabinet posts. These include Shukri Bishara, the new finance minister; Muhammad Mustafa, new deputy prime minister (who also has responsibility for economic affairs and heads the Palestine Investment Fund); Ziad Abu Amr, another new deputy prime minister; Said Abu Ali, the incumbent interior minister (who has nominal responsibility over certain branches of the PA security forces); and Riyad al Malki, the incumbent foreign minister. See, e.g., Daoud Kuttab, "Hamdallah's Complicated Job as Palestinian Prime Minister," *Al-Monitor Palestinian Pulse*, June 3, 2013.

[59] Khalil Shikaki of the Palestinian Center for Policy and Survey Research, a prominent Palestinian polling organization, quoted in Isabel Kershner, "End of Palestinian Power Play Muddles the Peace Process," *New York Times*, April 15, 2013.

[60] For additional details on the Gaza-Sinai dynamic, see CRS Report RL33003, *Egypt: Background and U.S. Relations*, by Jeremy M. Sharp.

[61] Given the reports of possibly reduced Iranian support in the wake of Hamas-Iran differences over the ongoing Syrian conflict, as discussed elsewhere in this report, it is unclear what current Iranian material support (if any) includes.

Until late 2010, Israeli and Egyptian authorities had closed most of Gaza's border crossings to everything but a minimum of goods deemed necessary to meet basic humanitarian needs, as a result of Hamas's forcible takeover of the territory.[62] This was ostensibly to deny Hamas materials to reconstitute its military capabilities, but it also prevented progress toward reinstituting pre-2007 living and working conditions. Hamas has bypassed Israeli restrictions and limitations on construction materials and dual-use items to some extent by encouraging and facilitating the expansion of a network of smuggling tunnels leading into Gaza from Egypt's Sinai Peninsula. Since 2011, Israeli relaxation of restrictions on imports and non-Israel/West Bank exports has facilitated renewed growth, but widespread unemployment and poverty persist.

In many respects, UNRWA and other international organizations and non-governmental organizations take care of the day-to-day humanitarian needs of many of Gaza's 1.8 million residents. Hamas's record of internal governance appears mixed. Anecdotes suggest efforts by the Hamas-led regime in some cases to more broadly project Islamic norms on Gazan society, as well as some efforts to show restraint. Polls indicate that Gazans tend to have a less positive view of Hamas than West Bankers who have not experienced direct Hamas rule, but also that Gazans acknowledge Hamas's general success in establishing and maintaining law and order. Hamas and non-Hamas militants periodically fire rockets into Israeli territory despite regular cease-fires—often provoking or responding to Israeli military action within Gaza. Non-Hamas militants appear to have fulfilled a useful function for Hamas by providing it opportunities to tacitly permit or encourage attacks against Israel while avoiding direct responsibility. Even if Hamas's capacity to harm Israel has declined, it might calculate that its militia deters challenges from other armed groups in Gaza, and that engaging in its own periodic attacks or rocket fire against Israeli targets maintains its "resistance credentials."

Hamas's control of Gaza presents a conundrum for Fatah, Israel, and the international community. They have not figured out how to assist Gaza's population without bolstering Hamas.[63] Breaking the political deadlock on Gaza could include one or more of the following: (1) actually implementing a political reunification of Gaza with the West Bank under a Palestinian factional power-sharing arrangement, (2) a general opening of Gaza's borders, (3) a formal Hamas-Israel truce. There are concerns that if the status quo holds, the massive unemployment and dispiriting living conditions that have persisted and at points worsened since Israel's withdrawal in 2005 could contribute to further radicalization of the population, decreasing prospects for peace with Israel and for Palestinian unity and increasing the potential for future violence. Israel disputes the level of legal responsibility for Gaza's residents that some international actors claim it retains—given its continued control of most of Gaza's borders, airspace, maritime access, and various buffer zones within the territory.

The Egyptian military has actively disrupted key aspects of Hamas's control over Gaza since it regained political control in Egypt in July 2013 and subsequently dispatched forces to counter an insurgency in the Sinai Peninsula. The military's efforts to significantly curtail the use of Gaza-Sinai smuggling tunnels has contributed to energy shortages and to spikes in unemployment and

---

[62] In November 2005, Israel and the PA signed an Agreement on Movement and Access, featuring U.S. and European Union participation in the travel and commerce regime that was supposed to emerge post-Gaza disengagement, but this agreement was never fully implemented. In September 2007, three months after Hamas's takeover of Gaza, the closure regime was further formalized when Israel declared Gaza to be a "hostile entity."

[63] See, e.g., Ibrahim Barzak and Karin Laub, "Hamas entrenched in Gaza after 5 years of rule," *Associated Press*, June 23, 2012.

prices in Gaza, which in turn has increased pressure on Hamas to address these developments.[64] In a January 2014 *Reuters* interview, unnamed Egyptian security officials outlined a plan that would apparently provide logistical support to Fatah and other anti-Hamas groups in Gaza.[65] Egypt's government alleges links between Hamas and militant groups in Sinai—such as Ansar Beit al Maqdis[66]—that have been stepping up attacks in Egypt in recent months. It is unclear, however, that Egypt is willing or able to decisively influence political outcomes in Gaza. An Israeli journalist writing on dynamics between Hamas, Egypt, and Israel stated:

> Israeli authorities are reluctant to push Hamas to the brink of collapse for fear of the unknown: namely, who would replace Hamas if its regime were brought down by mass protests? Israelis are concerned about anarchy erupting in the strip or, perhaps worse, a takeover by even more radical actors such as Iran-backed Palestinian Islamic Jihad or Salafi jihadists.[67]

Some observers speculate that, at least partly due to pressure it feels on its rule in Gaza, Hamas might be willing to provide concessions to Fatah as part of a reunification of the West Bank and Gaza.[68] It is unclear whether Hamas's apparent decision to engage in or permit increased rocket fire from Gaza in January 2014 after a long period of general quiet is indicative of a primarily defensive or aggressive posture. Egyptian, Israeli, and Fatah political, economic, and military measures—possibly taken in consultation or concert with U.S. policymakers—could significantly influence Hamas's future actions.

---

[64] Christa Case Bryant and Ahmed Aldabba, "As Egypt squeezes Gaza, Hamas looks increasingly cornered," *Christian Science Monitor*, January 21, 2014.

[65] Yasmine Saleh, "Exclusive - With Muslim Brotherhood crushed, Egypt sets sights on Hamas," *Reuters*, January 14, 2014. Hamas reportedly quashed attempts by some Gazans in 2013 to replicate the Tamarud ("rebellion" in Arabic) movement that helped lead to the ouster of Muhammad Morsi as Egypt's president, but Egypt reportedly hosted a Palestinian Tamarud conference in early January 2014. Ibid.

[66] See, e.g., "Profile: Egypt's militant Ansar Beit al-Maqdis group," *BBC News*, January 24, 2014.

[67] Ehud Yaari, "The New Triangle of Egypt, Israel, and Hamas," Washington Institute for Near East Policy, PolicyWatch 2193, January 17, 2014.

[68] Ibid.

Appendix A. Key Palestinian Factions and Groups

Palestine Liberation Organization (PLO)

The Palestine Liberation Organization (PLO) is recognized by the United Nations (including Israel since 1993) as the sole legitimate representative of the Palestinian people, wherever they may reside. It is an umbrella organization that includes 10 Palestinian factions (but not Hamas or other Islamist groups). As described above, the PLO was founded in 1964, and, since 1969, has been dominated by the secular nationalist Fatah movement. Organizationally, the PLO consists of an Executive Committee,[69] the Palestinian National Council (or PNC, its legislature), and a Central Council.[70]

After waging guerrilla warfare against Israel throughout the 1970s and 1980s under the leadership of the late Yasser Arafat from exile in Jordan, Lebanon, and Tunisia, the PNC declared Palestinian independence and statehood in 1988. This came at a point roughly coinciding with the PLO's decision to publicly accept the "land-for-peace" principle of U.N. Security Council Resolution 242 and to contemplate recognizing Israel's right to exist. The declaration had little practical effect, however, because the PLO was in exile in Tunisia and did not define the territorial scope of its state.[71] Nevertheless, the PLO refers to its Executive Committee chairman as the "President of the State of Palestine." The PLO recognized the right of Israel to exist in 1993 upon the signing of the Declaration of Principles (Oslo Accord) between the two parties.

While the PA maintains a measure of self-rule over various areas of the West Bank, as well as a legal claim to self-rule over Gaza despite its Hamas-led de facto regime,[72] the PLO remains the representative of the Palestinian people in negotiations with Israel and with other international actors. The PLO has a representative in Washington, DC (although it is not considered a formal diplomatic mission). Under the name "Palestine," the PLO is a member of UNESCO, maintains a permanent observer mission to the United Nations in New York and in Geneva as a "non-member state," and has missions and embassies in other countries—some with full diplomatic status. The PLO also is a full member of both the Arab League and the Organization of Islamic Cooperation.

[69] In addition to Abbas, the PLO Executive Committee includes such figures as Yasser Abed Rabbo, Saeb Erekat, Ahmed Qurei, and Hanan Ashrawi. A full listing can be found in "Abbas shuffles PLO Executive Committee, ousts Qaddoumi," *Ma'an*, September 14, 2009.

[70] The PNC is supposed to meet every two years to conduct business, and consists of approximately 700 members, a majority of whom are from the diaspora. The PNC elects the 18 members of the Executive Committee, who function as a cabinet—with each member assuming discrete responsibilities—and the Executive Committee elects its own chairperson. In August 2009, the PNC convened for the first time since 1998 when Mahmoud Abbas (Chairman of the PLO Executive Committee) called an extraordinary session in Ramallah to hold new Executive Committee elections. The Central Council is chaired by the PNC president and has over 100 members—consisting of the entire Executive Committee, plus (among others) representatives from Fatah and other PLO factions, the Palestinian Legislative Council, and prominent interest groups and professions. The Central Council functions as a link between the Executive Committee and the PNC that makes policy decisions between PNC sessions. See http://www.mideastweb.org/ palestianparties htm#PLO as a source for much of the PLO organizational information in this paragraph.

[71] The declaration included the phrase: "The State of Palestine is the state of Palestinians wherever they may be." The text is available at http://www.mideastweb.org/plc1988 htm.

[72] The PA's legal claim to self-rule over Gaza is subject both to the original Oslo-era agreements of the 1990s and to the agreements between Israel and the PA regarding movement and access that were formalized in November 2005 shortly after Israel's withdrawal from Gaza. The Hamas-led de facto regime maintains the legal claim that it exercises legal PA authority in both Gaza and the West Bank because of Hamas's 2006 legislative election victory.

Fatah

Fatah, the secular nationalist movement formerly led by Yasser Arafat, has been the largest and most prominent faction in the PLO for decades. Since the establishment of the PA and limited self-rule in the West Bank and Gaza in 1994, Fatah has dominated the PA, except during the period of Hamas rule of government ministries and the PLC in 2006-2007. Yet, problems with internecine violence, widespread disenchantment with Fatah's corruption and poor governance, and the failure to establish a Palestinian state have led to popular disillusionment. The death of Arafat in 2004 removed a major Fatah unifying symbol, further eroding the movement's support as Mahmoud Abbas took over its leadership.

Additionally, the image of Fatah as the embodiment of Palestinian nationalism and resistance to Israeli occupation has gradually faded away. Although he is the head of the movement, Mahmoud Abbas generally carries out his PLO and PA leadership roles without close consultation with his nominal allies in Fatah. In a November 2009 report, the International Crisis Group said, in reference to Fatah's seemingly declining influence:

> Resistance in the region is spearheaded by Islamic, not secular groups; Arafat is no more; diplomacy is President Abbas's preserve; Salam Fayyad's government dominates the West Bank, while Hamas controls Gaza. Far from being a big tent under which all Palestinian forces assemble, Fatah is being crowded out by competing forces.[73]

For years, analysts have pointed to a split within Fatah between those of the "old guard" (mainly Arafat's close associates from the period of exile) and those of a "young guard" some believe to be more attuned to on-the-ground realities—personified by leaders such as the imprisoned (by Israel) but popular Marwan Barghouti. Cleavages and overlaps within and among these groups and the political coming-of-age of even younger Fatah partisans, combined with factors mentioned above that have eroded Fatah's support base and credibility, have created doubts regarding Fatah's long-term cohesion and viability.

Fatah's 1960s charter has never been purged of its clauses calling for the destruction of the Zionist state and its economic, political, military, and cultural supports.[74] Abbas routinely expresses support for "legitimate peaceful resistance" to Israeli occupation under international law, complemented by negotiations. However, some of the other Fatah Central Committee members are either less outspoken in their advocacy of nonviolent resistance than Abbas, or reportedly explicitly insist on the need to preserve the option of armed struggle.[75]

---

[73] International Crisis Group, *Palestine: Salvaging Fatah*, Middle East Report No. 91, November 12, 2009.

[74] This is the case even though Fatah is the predominant member faction of the PLO, and the PLO formally recognized Israel's right to exist pursuant to the "Letters of Mutual Recognition" of September 9, 1993 (although controversy remains over whether the PLO charter has been amended to accommodate this recognition).

[75] Itamar Marcus and Nan Jacques Zilberdik, Palestinian Media Watch Bulletin (translating and quoting various Arabic-language sources), January 18, 2011; Samuel Sokol, "Senior Palestinian Official Backtracks on 'End' of Israel Remarks," *Algemeiner*, September 26, 2011. The Al Aqsa Martyrs' Brigades is a militant offshoot of Fatah that emerged in the West Bank early in the second intifada and later began operating in Gaza as well. The group initially targeted only Israeli soldiers and settlers, but in 2002 began a spate of attacks on civilians in Israeli cities and in March 2002 was added to the State Department's list of Foreign Terrorist Organizations. According to terrorism experts, the group switched tactics to restore Fatah's standing among Palestinians at a time when Palestinian casualties were mounting, Hamas's popularity was rising, and Fatah was tainted by its cooperation with Israel during the Oslo years. Most of the Brigades' members were believed to have hailed from the Palestinian security forces. As part of the Fatah-led PA's effort to centralize control over West Bank security since Hamas's takeover of Gaza in mid-2007, the (continued...)

Other PLO Factions and Leaders

Factions other than Fatah within the PLO include secular groups such as the Popular Front for the Liberation of Palestine (PFLP, a U.S.-designated Foreign Terrorist Organization), the Democratic Front for the Liberation of Palestine, and the Palestinian People's Party. All of these factions have minor political support relative to Fatah and Hamas.

A number of Palestinian politicians and other leaders without traditional factional affiliation have successfully gained followings domestically and in the international community under the PLO's umbrella, even some who are not formally affiliated with the PLO. Although these figures—such as Salam Fayyad, Hanan Ashrawi (a female Christian), and Mustafa Barghouti—often have competing agendas, several of them support a negotiated two-state solution, generally oppose violence, and appeal to the Palestinian intellectual elite and to prominent Western governments and organizations.

Hamas and Other Non-PLO Factions

Hamas

Overview

No Palestinian movement has benefitted more from, or contributed more to, Fatah's weakening than Hamas, which is an Arabic acronym for the "Islamic Resistance Movement." Hamas, for many years the main Palestinian opposition force, grew out of the Muslim Brotherhood, a religious and political organization founded in Egypt in 1928 with branches throughout the Arab world. Since Hamas's inception, it has maintained its primary base of support and particularly strong influence in the Gaza Strip. This influence has increased since Hamas's political bureau was compelled to relocate from Syria in early 2012 following its break with the Asad regime as a result of the violent approach the regime took in seeking—unsuccessfully—to quell the ongoing popular uprising.

Hamas combines Palestinian nationalism with Islamic fundamentalism. Its founding charter commits the group to the destruction of Israel and the establishment of an Islamic state in all of historic Palestine.[76] Written in 1988, Hamas's charter is explicit about the struggle for Palestine being a religious obligation. It describes the land as a *waqf*, or religious endowment, saying that no one can "abandon it or part of it." It calls for the elimination of Israel and Jews from Islamic holy land and portrays the Jews in decidedly negative terms, citing anti-Semitic texts. Some Hamas leaders have stated a conditional willingness to accept a long-term truce with Israel and a Palestinian state that does not include all of historic Palestine. However, some observers maintain that a decisive majority of Hamas members are unwilling to deviate from core principles of the

---

(...continued)

Brigades have (mainly voluntarily, partly through various amnesty programs) disbanded or at least lowered its profile in the West Bank.

[76] For the English translation of the 1988 Hamas charter, see http://avalon.law.yale.edu/20th_century/hamas.asp.

movement—namely, its ability to resort to violence and its unwillingness to agree to a permanent peace or territorial compromise with Israel.[77]

Hamas, along with several other major non-PLO factions that conditionally or absolutely reject the concept of peace with Israel, reportedly receives much of its political and material support from Iran. However, Iran appears to have significantly decreased its funding of Hamas due to its unwillingness to support the Asad regime in Syria,[78] Probably responding in part to widespread Palestinian disdain for Iran due to Iran's support for actions targeting Syria's Sunni-majority population and opposition groups, Hamas distanced itself from the Asad regime by abandoning its long-time external headquarters in Damascus in early 2012.[79]

Hamas has a variety of movement-wide and regional leadership organs. It is not entirely clear who controls overall strategy, policy, and financial decisions, especially given the politburo's loss of a centralized, Iran-linked headquarters-in-exile following its early 2012 departure from Damascus. Overall policy guidance comes from a Shura Council, with reported representation from major constituent areas inside and outside the West Bank and Gaza. In the past decade, the politburo approved a more direct role for Hamas in Palestinian politics while reportedly maintaining a variety of funding sources and a militia armed largely by Iran.

Hamas increased in popularity during the first two decades of its existence among many Palestinians apparently because of its reputation as a less corrupt provider of social services than Fatah and because of the image it cultivates of resistance to Israeli occupation. Fatah's political standing among Palestinians has been undermined by the inability of the PLO to induce Hamas to moderate its core principles (discussed above) in return for a more formalized role in national leadership organs.

Hamas's politicization and militarization can be traced to the first intifada that began in the Gaza Strip in 1987. Hamas's founder and spiritual leader, the late Sheikh Ahmed Yassin, established Hamas as the Muslim Brotherhood's local political arm in December 1987, following the eruption of the intifada.[80] Hamas rejected the Israel-PLO agreements of the mid-1990s, boycotted the 1996 elections, and has waged an intermittent terrorist campaign to undermine the peace process and opportunities for its resumption. Its military wing, the Izz Al Din al Qassam Brigades,[81] has killed more than 400 Israelis.[82] The State Department designated Hamas as a Foreign Terrorist

---

[77] CRS interview in September 2010 with U.S. analyst covering Middle East terrorism at major Washington, DC think tank. See Steven Erlanger, "Academics View Differences Within Hamas," *New York Times*, January 29, 2006.

[78] Nidal al-Mughrabi, "Foreign Funds for Hamas Hit by Syria Unrest-Diplomats," *Reuters*, August 21, 2011. Since this report, multiple Hamas leaders have visited Iran and received general promises of support, but the specific details of this support have remained vague. "Iran promises Hamas support during Zahar visit," *jpost.com*, March 15, 2012.

[79] Hamas's external leaders relocated to various countries within the region, with the two most visible personalities— Khaled Meshaal, the political bureau chief, and his deputy Musa Abu Marzouk—reportedly moving to Doha, Qatar and Cairo, respectively.

[80] Yassin had established the Islamic Center in Gaza in 1973. In subsequent years leading up to the intifada, Yassin's and his associates' activities—which led to Hamas's founding—were countenanced and sometimes supported by Israel, which believed the Islamists to be a convenient foil for the secular nationalist factions such as Fatah that Israel then perceived to be greater threats.

[81] Izz Al Din al Qassam was a Muslim Brotherhood member, preacher, and leader of an anti-Zionist and anti-British resistance movement during the Mandate period. He was killed by British forces on November 19, 1935.

[82] Figures culled from http://www.mfa.gov.il/MFA/Terrorism-+Obstacle+to+Peace/Palestinian+terror+before+2000/ Suicide%20and%20Other%20Bombing%20Attacks%20in%20Israel%20Since and http://www.mfa.gov.il/MFA/ Terrorism-+Obstacle+to+Peace/Palestinian+terror+since+2000/
(continued...)

Organization (FTO) in 1997 in response to its perpetration of suicide bombings against Israeli civilians, and U.S. aid to the Palestinians has been tailored to bypass Hamas and Hamas-controlled entities. Many of Hamas's leaders, including Sheikh Yassin, have been assassinated by Israel.[83]

Recent Developments and the Future

Hamas's future direction could depend largely on where it looks within the region for external support. If it continues past practices, it would rely on Iran for weapons, training, and some funding, while receiving other funding through a network of charitable organizations believed to be largely financed by private donors from Gulf states. Reliance on these sources, however, might change if Hamas emphasizes political and social activities over its military endeavors. Until mid-2013, Hamas apparently regarded Muslim Brotherhood groups in Egypt and elsewhere as possible alternative nodes of support to Iran. However, the July 2013 ouster of Muslim Brotherhood figure Muhammad Morsi as Egypt's president and the Egyptian military's subsequent efforts to counter Hamas's influence and presence in Egypt have reduced Hamas's external support options.[84]

In recent years, reports have indicated that Hamas leaders based outside Gaza might be seeking to move toward more nonviolent resistance in exchange for a significant role in the PLO and PA. However, external leaders might face obstacles to siphoning bureaucratic and popular support away from Gaza-based leaders without more control over funding streams or an on-the-ground presence. Historically, groups splitting from Palestinian Muslim Brotherhood-inspired movements—such as Palestine Islamic Jihad and several of Gaza's other militant groups—have gone in the other direction, seeking a more radical and violent approach.

Other Rejectionist Groups

Several other small Palestinian groups continue to reject the PLO's decision to recognize Israel's right to exist and to negotiate a two-state solution. They remain active in the West Bank and Gaza and retain some ability to carry out terrorist attacks and other forms of violence to undermine efforts at cooperation and conciliation. Their activities sometimes complicate the challenges the Fatah-led PA and Hamas authorities, respectively, face in maintaining security and internal order in the West Bank and Gaza—especially when Gaza rocket attacks provoke Israeli reprisals. In Gaza, some observers speculate that Hamas permits or even supports some of these groups, including those which have presences in the Sinai Peninsula and have been attacking targets in Egypt in recent months, without avowing ties to these groups.

(...continued)

Victims+of+Palestinian+Violence+and+Terrorism+sinc htm; and http://www.jewishvirtuallibrary.org/jsource/Terrorism/victims.html. In the aggregate, other Palestinian militant groups (such as Palestine Islamic Jihad – Shaqaqi Faction, the Fatah-affiliated Al Aqsa Martyrs' Brigades, and the Popular Front for the Liberation of Palestine) also have killed scores, if not hundreds, of Israelis since 1993.

[83] Israel assassinated Yassin (a quadriplegic confined to a wheelchair) on March 22, 2004, using helicopter-fired missiles, and then assassinated his successor in Gaza, Abdel Aziz al Rantissi, in the same manner less than one month later.

[84] Qatar may provide some material support, and Turkey is politically supportive.

Palestine Islamic Jihad – Shaqaqi Faction (PIJ)

The largest of these other groups is Palestine Islamic Jihad – Shaqaqi Faction (PIJ), a U.S.-designated Foreign Terrorist Organization that, like Hamas, is an offshoot of the Muslim Brotherhood and receives support from Iran. PIJ's secretary-general since 1995 has been Ramadan Abdullah Muhammad Shallah, who is reportedly based in Damascus, Syria. Since 2000, PIJ has conducted several attacks against Israeli targets (including over 30 suicide bombings), killing scores of Israelis.[85] PIJ, estimated at a few hundred members, emerged in the 1980s in the Gaza Strip as a rival to Hamas. Inspired by the Iranian revolution, it combined Palestinian nationalism, Sunni Islamic fundamentalism, and Shiite revolutionary thought. PIJ seeks liberation of all of historic Palestine through armed revolt and the establishment of an Islamic state, but unlike Hamas has not established a social services network, formed a political movement, or participated in elections. Mainly for these reasons, PIJ has never approached the same level of support among Palestinians as Hamas.

Popular Front for the Liberation of Palestine-General Command (PFLP-GC)

Another—though smaller—Iran-sponsored militant group designated as an FTO is the Popular Front for the Liberation of Palestine-General Command (PFLP-GC). PFLP-GC is a splinter group from the PFLP and has a following among Palestinian refugees in Lebanon and Syria. PFLP-GC's founder and secretary-general is Ahmed Jibril. He is reportedly based in Damascus and allied with the Asad regime.

Popular Resistance Committees

The Popular Resistance Committees (PRC) is a loose alliance of armed dissidents and militants that first appeared in the Gaza Strip in 2000.[86] Israel reportedly claims that the PRC receives some material support from Hezbollah. The membership of the PRC encompasses both secular and Islamist Palestinian movements, including Fatah, Hamas, and the PFLP. The group was implicated in the October 15, 2003, attack that killed three U.S. diplomatic security personnel in the Gaza Strip.[87] In part to avenge the Israeli killing of the PRC's founder, Jamal Abu Samhadana, in June 2006 the PRC (along with Hamas and a splinter group calling itself the Army of Islam) launched the raid on an Israeli army post near the Gaza Strip that captured Israeli soldier Gilad Shalit and killed two of Shalit's comrades.[88] The PRC's secretary general, Zuhair al Qaissi, was killed in an Israeli air strike in March 2012.

---

[85] See footnote 38.

[86] An Israeli source on the PRC is The Meir Amit Intelligence and Information Center, "The Popular Resistance Committees: Portrait of the Terrorist Organization Responsible for the Series of Combined Terrorist Attacks North of Eilat, Israel's Southernmost City," August 23, 2011.

[87] See Conal Urquhart, Chris McGreal, and Suzanne Goldenberg, "Palestinians bomb US convoy," *Guardian* (UK), October 16, 2003. The PRC claimed, and then later denied, responsibility for the attack, a roadside bomb that destroyed the van in which the men were traveling.

[88] Shalit was freed in 2011, through Egyptian-mediated negotiations between Hamas and Israel, in exchange for more than 1,000 Palestinian prisoners.

Salafist Militant Groups

A number of small but potentially growing Palestinian Salafist fundamentalist militant groups with an affinity for Al Qaeda-style ideology and tactics have arisen in the Gaza Strip.[89] Such groups operating in Gaza or in Sinai with possible links to Gaza militants (including Hamas) include the Army of Islam, Ansar Beit al Maqdis, Mujahadeen Shura Council in the Environs of Jerusalem, Ansar al Jihad, and Tawhid (Monotheism) and Jihad. Some Salafist groups reportedly include several former Hamas militia commanders who have become disaffected with Hamas's informal cease-fires with Israel and other actions they perceive as having moderated Hamas's stance. They do not currently appear to threaten Hamas's rule in Gaza. Yet, with enough influential adherents or outside support, these groups could possibly either pressure Hamas to renew active confrontation with Israel or pose a long-term challenge to its rule, either directly or by provoking action from Egypt or Israel.

Palestinian Refugees

In General

Of the some 700,000 Palestinians displaced during the 1947-1948 Arab-Israeli war, about one third ended up in the West Bank, one third in the Gaza Strip, and one third in neighboring Arab countries. They and their descendants now number approximately 5 million, with roughly one-third living in refugee camps in the West Bank, Gaza, Jordan, Lebanon, and Syria. Jordan offered Palestinian refugees citizenship, partly owing to its previous unilateral annexation of the West Bank (which ended in 1988), but the other refugees in the region are stateless and therefore limited in their ability to travel. Refugees receive little or no assistance from Arab host governments and many (including those who do not live in camps) remain reliant on the U.N. Relief and Works Agency for Palestine Refugees in the Near East (UNRWA) for food, health care, and/or education. For additional information on UNRWA (including historical U.S. contributions) and recent congressional action concerning it, see CRS Report RS22967, *U.S. Foreign Aid to the Palestinians*, by Jim Zanotti.

For many years, Congress has raised concerns about how to ensure that UNRWA funds are used for the programs it supports and not for terrorist activities or corrupt purposes. Refugee camps are not controlled or policed by UNRWA, but by the host countries or governing authorities.[90] Concerns also have been expressed about the content of textbooks and educational materials used by UNRWA, with claims that they promote anti-Semitism and exacerbate tensions between Israelis and Palestinians. UNRWA responds that the host country, not UNRWA, provides the textbooks and determines their content because students must take exams in host country degree programs. Additionally, UNRWA integrates human rights-themed education into its school programs for both teachers and students.[91]

For political and economic reasons, Arab host governments generally have not actively supported the assimilation of Palestinian refugees into their societies. Even if able to assimilate, many Palestinian refugees hold out hope of returning to the homes they or their ancestors left behind or

---

[89] Tobias Buck, "Extremists pose growing threat in Gaza," *Financial Times*, April 18, 2011.

[90] UNRWA's responsibilities are limited to providing its services to refugees and administering its own installations.

[91] See http://www.unrwa.org/what-we-do/human-rights-promotion?program=33.

possibly to a future Palestinian state. According to many observers, it is difficult to overstate the deep sense of dispossession and betrayal refugees feel over never having been allowed to return to their homes, land, and property. Some Palestinian factions have organized followings among refugee populations, and militias have proliferated in some refugee areas outside of the Palestinian territories, particularly in Lebanon.[92] Thus, the refugees exert significant pressure on both their host governments and the Palestinian leadership in the West Bank and Gaza to seek a solution to their claims as part of any final status deal with Israel.

Effects of Syria Conflict

The growing endangerment of Palestinian refugees in Syria as its internal conflict continues could have implications both on developments there and for factional politics in the West Bank and Gaza. According to UNRWA Deputy Commissioner-General Margot Ellis as of January 23, 2014, of about 540,000 Palestinian refugees registered in Syria, approximately half "are displaced in Syria, and another 80,000 are dispersed in the region and beyond."[93] Of those dispersed, UNRWA reports:

> Fifty-one thousand have reached Lebanon, 11,000 have identified themselves in Jordan, 5,000 are in Egypt, and smaller numbers have reached Gaza, Turkey and further afield. Those who have reached Lebanon, Jordan and Egypt face risky legal limbo compounded with living conditions so difficult that many decide to return to the dangers inside Syria.[94]

Yarmouk refugee camp in Damascus, which used to be home to more than 160,000 Palestinian refugees, now reportedly has around 18,000 after being caught in the conflict, and its residents have reportedly been cut off from regular shipments of food and medical aid for months.[95]

---

[92] A case in point is the small Palestinian-associated Islamist fundamentalist militant group known as Fatah al Islam. In 2007, Fatah al Islam was battled and eventually defeated by Lebanese security forces in and around Tripoli and the Nahr al Bared refugee camp. Numbering between 100 and 300, this group was variously described by some as being mainly Palestinian, and by others as more pan-Arab, and as having ties to Al Qaeda or to Syrian intelligence.

[93] The UNRWA Syria Regional Crisis Response Plan 2014: A Briefing on Recent Developments, January 23, 2014.

[94] Ibid. According to UNRWA's website, Jordan stemmed the flow of Palestinian refugees from Syria over its borders after announcing a policy of non-entry in early 2013.

[95] UNRWA news release: "UNRWA successfully delivers aid to Yarmouk," January 30, 2014; UN News Centre, "Syria: UN agency calls for urgent aid delivery to besieged Palestinian refugee camp," January 22, 2014. On January 30, 2014, UNRWA stated that it had been able to deliver food to some families inside Yarmouk, but also stated that it was seeking authorization and support for continued access to the camp in order to provide food for the entire civilian population. UNRWA news release, op. cit. Reportedly, much of the fighting in Yarmouk has taken place between opposition factions and Asad regime-allied PFLP-GC operatives. "'Aid enters' besieged Damascus camp of Yarmouk," *BBC News*, January 18, 2014.

Appendix B. Key Palestinian Leaders

Mahmoud Abbas (aka "Abu Mazen")—Fatah

Born in 1935 in Safed in what is now northern Israel, Abbas and his family left as refugees for Syria in 1948 when Israel was founded. He earned a B.A. in law from Damascus University and a Ph.D. in history from Moscow's Oriental Institute.[96] Abbas was an early member of Yasser Arafat's Fatah movement, joining in Qatar, and became a top deputy to Arafat and head of the PLO's national and international relations department in 1980. Abbas initiated dialogue with Jewish and pacifist movements as early as the 1970s, and, as the head of the Palestinian negotiating team to the secret Oslo talks in the early 1990s, is widely seen as one of the main architects of the peace process.[97]

Abbas returned to the Palestinian territories in September 1995 and took residences in Gaza and Ramallah. Together with Yossi Beilin (then an Israeli Labor Party government minister), Abbas drafted a controversial "Framework for the Conclusion of a Final Status Agreement Between Israel and the PLO" (better known as the "Abu Mazen-Beilin Plan") in October 1995.[98] In March 2003, Abbas was named the first PA prime minister, but never was given full authority because Arafat (the PA president) insisted that ultimate decision-making authority and control over security services lie with him. Abbas resigned as prime minister in frustration with Arafat, the United States, and Israel in September 2003.

Following the death of Yasser Arafat in November 2004, Abbas succeeded Arafat as chairman of the PLO's Executive Committee, and he won election as Arafat's successor as PA president in January 2005 with 62% of the vote. His presidency has been marked by events that include Israel's 2005 unilateral withdrawal from Gaza; the January 2006 Hamas legislative electoral victory; the June 2007 Hamas takeover of Gaza; the 2007-2008 U.S.-supported Annapolis negotiating process with Israeli Prime Minister Ehud Olmert; unsuccessful PLO insistence on a complete Israeli settlement freeze in 2009-2010; attempts in 2011-2012 to gain greater international recognition of Palestinian statehood; and renewed negotiations with Israel since 2013. Many reports indicate that Abbas has taken several actions and positions reluctantly, and is motivated by a complex combination of factors that include resisting challenges to his personal authority, preventing destabilization and violence, and maintaining as many political and diplomatic options as possible. Some observers allege that his rule is becoming increasingly authoritarian and corrupt.

---

[96] Some Jewish groups allege that Abbas's doctoral thesis and a book based on the thesis (entitled ▢▢e ▢▢e▢▢e▢▢e ▢e▢▢e▢▢e▢▢▢▢s▢▢▢Be▢wee▢N▢▢s▢ ▢▢▢▢▢▢s▢) downplayed the number of Holocaust victims and accused Jews of collaborating with the Nazis. Abbas has maintained that his work merely cited differences between other historians on Holocaust victim numbers, and has stated that "The Holocaust was a terrible, unforgivable crime against the Jewish nation, a crime against humanity that cannot be accepted by humankind." "Profile: Mahmoud Abbas," *BBC News*.

[97] Yet, one of the Black September assassins involved in the 1972 Munich Olympics terrorist attack that killed 11 Israeli athletes has claimed that Abbas was responsible for financing the attack, even though Abbas "didn't know what the money was being spent for." Alexander Wolff, "The Mastermind," ▢▢▢s ▢▢▢s▢▢▢e▢, August 26, 2002.

[98] The Abu Mazen-Beilin plan contemplated a two-state solution that, among other things, would create a special mechanism for governing Jerusalem that would allow it to function as the capital of both Israel and Palestine, and would resolve the Palestinian refugee issue by allowing return to Israel only in special cases and providing for a compensation regime and resettlement elsewhere in most others. Its existence was denied for five years until its text was made public in 2000. Text available at http://www.bitterlemons.org/docs/beilinmazen.html.

Khaled Meshaal—Hamas[99]

Khaled Meshaal, based in Doha, Qatar, is the chief of Hamas's political bureau. He was named a specially designated global terrorist (SDGT) by the Treasury Department in August 2003.

Born in 1956 near Ramallah in the West Bank, Meshaal (alternate spellings: Mishal, Mashal) moved with his family to Jordan in 1967 following Israel's occupation of the West Bank in the June Arab-Israeli ("Six-Day") War. As a student and schoolteacher in Kuwait, he became a leader in the Palestinian Islamist movement. After the founding of Hamas in 1987, Meshaal led the Kuwaiti branch of the organization, then moved to Jordan in 1991 after Iraq's invasion of Kuwait. He took over as Hamas politburo chief following the 1995 U.S. arrest of then chief Musa Abu Marzouk, who was released in 1997 and now serves as Meshaal's Cairo-based deputy.

In September 1997, Meshaal was targeted in Amman by the Mossad (Israel's foreign intelligence service) in an assassination attempt that became a major international incident. This culminated in King Hussein of Jordan threatening to abrogate the 1994 Israel-Jordan peace treaty in order to get Binyamin Netanyahu (in his first stint as Israeli prime minister) to supply an antidote to the nerve toxin to which Meshaal had been exposed.[100] After the Hamas leadership was expelled from Jordan in November 1999, Meshaal first moved to Doha, Qatar, then settled two years later in Damascus, Syria, where he was based until the ongoing civil conflict led to the relocation of Hamas's external leadership in early 2012.

Meshaal became acknowledged as Hamas's overall leader in 2004, following the assassination of Abdel Aziz al Rantissi by Israel. Meshaal also serves as Hamas's top diplomat, often traveling and meeting with various governments and political leaders—including European legislators and former President Jimmy Carter. Reports indicate that Meshaal's leadership and influence within Hamas has been challenged in recent years. This may be partly because of disputes between Meshaal and his loyalists with several prominent Hamas leaders—including many based in Gaza—regarding Meshaal's perceived focus on political means of resistance at the expense of military means. Meshaal may also face challenges owing to the external leadership's reduced cohesion and control over various channels of influence and funding following its exile from Damascus.

Ismail Haniyeh—Hamas

Ismail Haniyeh is Hamas's "prime minister" in Gaza.

Haniyeh was born in or around 1955 in the Shati refugee camp in the Gaza Strip. In 1989, he was imprisoned for three years by Israeli authorities for participation in the first ▯▯▯▯▯▯. Following his release in 1992, he was deported to Lebanon along with approximately 400 other Hamas activists, but was eventually allowed to return to Gaza in 1993. Upon his return, he was appointed dean of the Islamic University, and became the leader of Hamas's student movement. He was closely associated with Hamas co-founder and spiritual leader Sheikh Ahmed Yassin, and,

---

[99] See also "Khaled Mishal, external leader, Hamas Political Bureau," ▯▯e ▯s ▯▯e ▯▯▯e ▯▯e ▯ee▯▯, December 16, 2009.

[100] For a detailed account of the failed assassination attempt and Meshaal's rise to power within Hamas, see Paul McGeough, ▯▯▯▯▯▯▯▯▯▯▯e ▯▯▯e▯▯ ▯ss▯▯ss▯ss▯▯▯▯▯ ▯▯▯▯▯▯▯ ▯s▯▯▯▯▯▯e ▯se ▯▯▯▯▯s, New York: The New Press, 2009.

following the assassination of Yassin and much of the Hamas leadership in 2004, became a prominent Hamas leader in Gaza.

Haniyeh favored Hamas's participation in the 2006 PLC elections, and headed the Hamas list of candidates. Following Hamas's victory, he served as PA prime minister from March 2006 until June 2007. Following Hamas's takeover of Gaza and Abbas's dismissal of its ministers from the PA government in the West Bank, Hamas has continued to insist that Haniyeh is the PA prime minister, and he is treated as such in Gaza. In Palestinian opinion polls for hypothetical presidential elections, Haniyeh sometimes runs close to Mahmoud Abbas in head-to-head pairings.

Author Contact Information

Jim Zanotti
Specialist in Middle Eastern Affairs
jzanotti@crs.loc.gov, 7-1441

www.ingramcontent.com/pod-product-compliance
Lightning Source LLC
Chambersburg PA
CBHW080639290526
45790CB00007B/3129